How to Beat
Panic Disorder

One Step at a Time

Paul Farrand
and Marie Chellingsworth

ROBINSON

ROBINSON

First published in Great Britain in 2016 by Robinson

Copyright © Paul Farrand and Marie Chellingsworth, 2016

This book is not intended as a substitute for medical advice or treatment. Any person with a condition requiring medical attention should consult a qualified medical practitioner or suitable therapist.

A CIP catalogue record for this book
is available from the British Library.

ISBN 978-1-4721-0884-5

Typeset in Minion by Initial Typesetting Services, Edinburgh
Printed and bound in Great Britain by Clays Ltd, St Ives plc

Papers used by Robinson are from well-managed forests
and other responsible sources

MIX
Paper from
responsible sources
FSC® C104740

Robinson
is an imprint of
Little, Brown Book Group
Carmelite House
50 Victoria Embankment
London EC4Y 0DZ

An Hachette UK Company
www.hachette.co.uk

www.littlebrown.co.uk

CONTENTS

Section 1

GETTING GOING

Great start!

Sometimes the hardest steps are the first ones. Just by picking up this self-help book and beginning to read it, you have taken a big first step forwards. It is often very difficult to get going. So it's great you have taken the first step!

Things can be overwhelming and frightening when you have feelings of panic. In many cases these feelings may have had a wider range of impacts and consequences on your daily life. So we have written the book in short sections to enable you to work through it at a pace that suits you. We have also included examples, called 'case studies', of people who have used techniques in the book to understand and get back on top of their own feelings of panic they experienced. These show how they put the techniques they learned into action in their daily life to help with their feelings of panic. They have also provided us with some top tips to share with you about creating and using your own personal Toolkit of techniques.

They are honest accounts that show there are things you can do that will help. It is not always easy, and there is no quick fix. But by breaking things down, and doing them step by step, small changes can lead to bigger change.

Getting to know us

First of all we would like to introduce ourselves and let you know more about us and why we have written this book. We both work at universities teaching people to use CBT (Cognitive Behavioural Therapy) skills and we also work clinically with patients. CBT is an evidence-based treatment recommended for people experiencing panic attacks, panic disorder and for those with other anxiety difficulties and depression and is the approach used in this book. We have both taught many other practitioners to use CBT to help people and worked with the Department of Health to help set standards for the training and delivery of CBT in England.

Paul Farrand: I am an Associate Professor and Director of Post-Graduate Psychological Wellbeing Practitioner (PWPs) clinical training programmes within Clinical Education, Development and Research

(CEDAR) at the University of Exeter. I am a health psychologist and in my clinical work I practise Cognitive Behavioural Therapy, mainly working with people who experience a range of psychological difficulties alongside physical health problems. Most recently I worked with people in hospital with a range of psychological difficulties arising from problems with their head and neck. The focus of my research is upon developing and improving access to CBT interventions, most recently CBT self-help interventions for people with dementia and armed forces veterans. Outside of work I enjoy spending time with my wife Paula, and three children Oliver, Ellis and Amélie. We enjoy eating out and walking in the East Devon countryside and by the sea with our two black Labradors, Gus and Bing. I also have an interest in 1950s British cinema.

Marie Chellingsworth: I am Executive Director of CBT and Evidence-Based Psychologies at the University of East Anglia (UEA). Prior to this I was Director of training programmes for Psychological Wellbeing Practitioners (PWPs) and undergraduate Applied Psychology (Clinical) students at the universities of Nottingham and Exeter. I am passionate about CBT training for older people and ensuring people over the age of 65 get equal access to treatment and I have developed national curriculum and training materials for the IAPT programme. My clinical and research areas are adults with depression and anxiety disorders, dementia as well as improving the quality of clinical skills training. I am renovating an old 1800s lodge in Devon that I share with my Irish setters Alfie and Monty. Outside of work I love good music and spending time with friends. (My secret pleasure is watching *Emmerdale*!)

So what is Cognitive Behavioural Therapy?

This book is based on an evidence-based psychological therapy called Cognitive Behavioural Therapy, or CBT for short. CBT is recommended by the National Institute of Health and Care Excellence (NICE) as a psychological therapy for use within the NHS for people experiencing frequent panic attacks, often called panic disorder, several other anxiety difficulties, and depression. This recommendation is based on the findings of many research trials that show CBT is effective for lots of people with anxiety difficulties and depression. These recommendations cover CBT both when it is delivered face-to-face by a therapist and also when delivered in a CBT self-help format, such as the book you are now reading. Based on our own clinical experience we can personally recommend it for people experiencing the occasional panic attack, or panic disorder if they begin to be experienced far more frequently. We know how much CBT can help and we will explain more about how it works later in this section.

Using self-help

This book uses a self-help approach. It gives you the tools you can put into practice at a pace that suits you. Given the good evidence and NICE recommendations for CBT self-help, you may have come across it before and already be familiar with it. However, if this is your first experience of CBT self-help, initially it may seem a bit daunting flicking through this book. This is understandable and you may be wondering what lies ahead. We have worked hard making this book as easy as possible to read and use. To do this we have taken a lot of advice from people who have experienced panic attacks or panic disorder and followed good practice in writing self-help books.

How to use this book

The important thing to remember is that you don't need to tackle the book all at once. In fact we would recommend you didn't! One of the advantages of using self-help is that you can use it at a time that suits you, for a period of time that suits you and in a location that suits you. To help with this we have broken the book down into a number of sections, to enable you to use it over smaller periods of time. It may be that your healthcare practitioner recommended this self-help book and you will be using it together. If that is the case, they can answer any questions you may have and help you along the way. If not and you are reading this without a healthcare practitioner, you may wish to highlight helpful bits or make notes for yourself as you go along. Other people have told us this is really helpful. Remember if at any time you are not sure about something, you can go back and look at that part again.

Overview of the book

We have tried to make this self-help book as easy as possible for you to use. Some people like to read through things at first and then start using the techniques. Others prefer to start using the techniques straight away. Whatever suits you is fine. However, the key thing is to put the techniques into practice in your daily life. Work through the techniques at a pace that suits you and complete the activities as you go along. We have broken the book into five sections. You can move through the book in the way you feel will help you the most.

You may want to read about other people who have

experienced panic attacks or panic disorder and how this approach helped them. In Section 5 we have included two recovery stories. Here, Mike and Ria have kindly shared their stories and what they did to get on top of their panic. Some people like to read this first. Others prefer to read more about CBT and make their own plan first. Either way is fine.

Here are the five sections. You can move through these sections in the way you feel will help you the most.

Section 1: Getting going (page 1)

In this section, we will help you understand a little more about the feelings of panic you have been having and about something called panic disorder, alongside a discussion of treatments. There are stories and tips from other people who have used this approach to help you get started and keep going. You can set your goals to indicate where you want to be and help you know you are feeling better.

Section 2: Understanding panic attacks and panic disorder (page 27)

Here you will learn to appreciate how panic attacks or panic disorder are affecting you and we will show you how the tools included within the book can be really helpful.

Section 3: Panic diary and Exposure therapy
(page 63)

Using the tools within this self-help book, we will help you make your own plan to get on top of your panic. Then you can look at how to put this plan into action and review your progress.

Section 4: The Relapse Prevention Toolkit
(page 95)

When you are feeling better you will be supported to make a plan to keep on top of your panic in the future and stay well.

Section 5: Recovery Stories (page 125)

Finally, you can catch up again with the people you first met in Section 1. Here they have shared their stories of having panic attacks and panic disorder and discuss what they did to help themselves. You can see how they put their plans into action and continued to stay on top of their panic.

Top tips before you get going

Before beginning to understand panic attacks and panic disorder and the way they affect you, we would like to share some top tips about using self-help. These tips come from people who have used CBT self-help to overcome their emotional difficulties and from mental health professionals who support patients to use CBT self-help like this.

Top tip 1: Give it your best shot

'I really struggled getting motivated to begin with. I stuck with it and I'm so glad I did.'

As with any new activity, you may struggle at times when using this self-help book. But just give it your best shot; this is all anyone can ask of you. When things seem too much it can really help to read the case studies in Section 5 of people who have put things into action and got on top of their panic attacks or overcome their panic disorder. Revisiting the case studies at regular intervals can help to motivate you. If a healthcare practitioner is supporting you, then talking to them when you find things difficult can help. They can encourage and support you.

Top tip 2: Put what you learn into action

'When I started to manage my panic attacks better it really helped me look back on what I had done and had achieved.'

Even though you may not feel like it at first, putting the things you learn in this book into action is a key way for you to start feeling better. However, you don't need to do everything at once. Step-by-step, the book guides you through ways to break things down and put them into action in your daily life. Think about using this self-help book to help you get better a bit like the way someone works out in the gym to get fitter. Just having a gym membership card or a fitness-training programme from an instructor doesn't make you fitter straight away (if only!). The same applies to you getting over your panic attacks, or panic disorder. This self-help book is here to provide you with the tools to help you reach your goals. But you will only get the most from it if you then put those tools into action.

Top tip 3: Writing in the book is allowed. In fact we encourage it!

'Writing things down was really useful as it helped me take a step back from things. It was good to be able to look back and see how things were going in black and white. That way I couldn't talk myself out of the way things had improved!'

Unlike most books, CBT self-help books are designed to be written in, in fact the more the better! The more you interact with it and make it personal to you, the more it can help. To make this easier, each time there is something for you to write we have put in this image. When you see it, it is a sign for you to write in the book and make a plan. Writing things down can really help you achieve your plan and enable you to look back in the future and to see how far you have come.

Top tip 4: Like everyone, expect to have good days and bad days

'When I got over my panic disorder, I was so pleased I never wanted to take a step back. Then one day I was at work and had a panic attack at my desk. I thought my panic disorder had come back again and I would never get on top of it. I almost gave up. However, later that evening, I then re-membered to go back to the plan I had in place and used my "Panic Diary" to record the panic attack to try to understand it better. And I did, it was just my body natur-ally responding to my anxiety when I was given an interview date for a promotion. Understanding this helped me get back on track and in fact helped me understand much better the section of the book on "relapse prevention" I was just starting.'

After using this book for a few weeks you will better understand what panic attacks are and why anyone could experience one. You will also hopefully notice a gradual improve-ment in getting on top of them. However, as feelings of panic are perfectly normal at times and occasionally experienced by most people, you will most likely continue to have the odd one now and again. Just try and keep on track with your plan and avoid letting how you are feeling internally affect your use of this book and what you may have learned.

Top tip 5: Act according to your goals and targets, not because of how you feel and think inside

'The most powerful thing I learned is to act according to my goals, not how I am feeling internally or what I am thinking. Knowing this helped so much I have set it as a message on the screensaver on my laptop. This makes me more aware of when I am heading into a vicious panic cycle again and helps me break it before it takes hold.'

A main focus of this book is to act according to your goals and targets, not how you are thinking or especially feeling internally. You will therefore be asked to set some goals a bit later in this section. You will also read more about breaking your vicious panic cycle in Section 2. This is a key way to start to get on top of your panic attacks. So try not to listen to your body when you get these feelings of panic and don't let them stop you doing things you need to, or want to, as a result.

Top tip 6: Let your GP know you are going to use the book

'Although everyone was telling me I was having panic attacks and suggested I get treatment for them, which is when a friend recommended this book, I still felt a bit uneasy doing anything about them until I had discussed them with my GP. I felt a bit silly going back again but she was really helpful. In fact she said how pleased she was I was finally trying to get on top of my panic and was pleased this book was based on CBT, as there was a lot to recommend about CBT. She also said she was happy I spoke to her first. This was because some of the exercises would require me to try out some things that would actually make me experience the physical feelings I was so scared of. But she also said there were few reasons why the majority of people would experience any medical problems doing them, and no reasons why I couldn't do them. But I should get back in touch if I did. I found this advice really helpful, and it gave me confidence to give the book a go.'

There are no medical reasons to prevent you using the exercises in this self-help book, and the majority of people will not experience any problems with them. However, the exercises will ask you to do things that will simulate the type of panicky physical feelings that cause you so much distress. So we do recommend that you let your GP (or other healthcare provider if they know you better) aware before engaging with the 'exposure' activities in Section 3, just to be completely sure there are no problems.

Top tip 7: Involve family and friends if you can

'It really helped me when I discussed my panic attacks and how they made me feel with my wife. She really wanted to help, and convinced me to go to the doctor to begin with. After starting to use this book, I found showing it to her and reading it together helped her understand what I was struggling with and ways she could help me. It was really helpful she was around when I practised my quick breathing exercises for the first time. Not that anything went wrong, although at that time I was still convincing myself it would, and having Sue nearby helped me give them a go to begin with.'

There are many ways that just having others around, and involving them when you are using this self-book can be helpful.

The vast majority of people do not experience any difficulties and this type of intervention is the one recommended for people with panic attacks or panic disorder. Involving friends and family may help you use this self-help book in other ways too. For example by helping you to look at things differently, find ways to solve problems or simply be there for a chat. If you think you might find the support of others helpful and they are happy to help, then why not ask? If you show them this book, they may find the sections on panic attacks and panic disorder and how they are affecting you helpful. Sometimes having something for family members to read through can really help. So we have included a section at the back for family and carers to understand how to support you to use the book. If you think this may help, why not get them involved and ask them to read this section or discuss it together?

Top tip 8: Set aside time to use the book and set reminders to help you remember

'When I started using this, I set myself an alert twice a week in the diary on my computer and made sure I set time aside to work through the book sections and activities. Not putting them off and making the use of the book an equal priority to other things really helped. It was hard to get going as I was a little afraid, but so worth it when I got into the routine and then began to feel better. It was something my GP recommended I did.'

Many people, especially those with busy work or family lives, report struggling or forgetting to do things and this can get in the way of using the book. However, setting reminders for yourself in whatever ways are best for you may help. For example, computers and many mobile phones now have a diary function that allows you to put in activities for the week and alert you when you are due to do them. If you do not have these you may find putting sticky notes on your fridge or cupboard doors works just as well.

Getting and using support

At times you may feel like giving up using this book. Don't worry, it's perfectly normal to occasionally feel that way or have distressing thoughts because of your panic. These feelings will pass and you can keep in control by still doing your plan. Keeping going at these times, although challenging, will help you keep working towards feeling better and for many people being supported by someone helps them stay motivated and on track.

It may be that you are already receiving support from a GP or other healthcare practitioner. In several countries it is now even possible to receive support from a healthcare practitioner who is specially trained in motivating and supporting people to work through CBT self-help, such as this book. For example, the NHS in England have Improving Access to Psychological Therapies (IAPT) services, where people suitable for CBT self-help and struggling with anxiety or low mood can be supported face-to-face or over the telephone by a Psychological Wellbeing Practitioner (PWP). PWPs are healthcare practitioners who are specifically trained to motivate and support people to work through CBT self-help like this book. If you are receiving support it is likely you will speak to them regularly to help you identify and solve any problems and answer any questions you may have. In England, to find out about your local IAPT service go to:

http://www.iapt.nhs.uk/services/ www.

You may not be receiving support to use this book. Or you may live in an area where IAPT services are unavailable. You may, however, feel that you would benefit from some support. If this applies to you, talk to your GP, who may have access to other services that can offer support in your local area or who can recommend an accredited CBT therapist who works in your area. Equally, you may wish to work through this book alone or with a friend or family member. That is also fine. We know that research shows that having someone to support you use CBT can make it more effective.

There are no rules about how quickly you should work through this book. There are also no expectations about the amount of time it will take you to feel better. However, for the book to be successful we would ask you to commit to two things.

1. Give it a go: Read it and do it!

Give the activities a go to see what works for you. The more you can put things into practice, the more likely you will see the benefits. Remember we all have days we feel like giving upon things. Make a commitment to use the book *and* put things into practice, even if you are not sure it will work for you. Maybe make a deal with yourself to try it for six weeks and see how you feel.

2. If things get really bad and you think about ending your life, speak to someone straight away

For some people, but certainly not all, when they are experiencing emotional difficulties and things begin to get on top of them, they can feel so bad they think about ending their life and make plans towards this. If things get so bad that you are having these thoughts or start harming yourself in any way – get help now! There are details of support agencies you can contact 24 hours a day in the back of this book (pages 173–6). Let your GP or other healthcare worker know, they are there to help. Or tell someone else, such as a trusted friend or family member and they may be able to get help. Remember you won't always feel this way and there are things you can do to feel better.

Building motivation to change

We have worked with many people who have struggled to get going and have found the following activity can be helpful. Complete the box below to think about what your life will be like again if you did not experience panic attacks or panic disorder. You can write as much or as little as you like. Then we will help you to set some goals you want to work on.

Building Motivation to Change: The miracle question

Imagine after you go to sleep tonight a miracle happens and when you wake up everything in your life was how you wanted it to be and panic and anxiety are no longer a problem for you. Write down below what your life would look like if this miracle happened.

Thinking ahead

Over the page you have thought about what your life will be like if a miracle happened and you no longer suffered from feelings of panic. Now we would like you to think about getting there and achieving the life you want.

The way to do this is to break things down into more manageable goals you would like to achieve over the next few months. These may be things you have done in the past that you have stopped doing, or new things you would like to achieve in the future. Try and make these goals:

- Specific to you.

- Capable of being measured so you can record your progress.

- Realistic for you to achieve.

When you've decided on your goals for feeling better, rate each one regarding how far you can achieve that goal now, and then you can come back and re-rate them again in one, two and three months' time to measure your progress. OK, let's get started!

Rating my goals

My goals for feeling better

Goal 1: ....

....

.....................................Today's date___/___/___

I can do this now (circle a number):

0	1	2	3	4	5	6
Not at all		Occasionally		Often		Any time

One month re-rating   (Today's date___/___/___)
(circle a number):

0	1	2	3	4	5	6
Not at all		Occasionally		Often		Any time

Two month re-rating   (Today's date___/___/___)
(circle a number):

0	1	2	3	4	5	6
Not at all		Occasionally		Often		Any time

Three month re-rating   (Today's date___/___/___)
(circle a number):

    0   1   2   3   4   5   6
    Not at all   Occasionally   Often   Any time

Goal 2: ....

....

...............................Today's date___/___/___

I can do this now (circle a number):

    0   1   2   3   4   5   6
    Not at all   Occasionally   Often   Any time

One month re-rating   (Today's date___/___/___)
(circle a number):

    0   1   2   3   4   5   6
    Not at all   Occasionally   Often   Any time

Two month re-rating   (Today's date___/___/___)
(circle a number):

    0   1   2   3   4   5   6
    Not at all   Occasionally   Often   Any time

Three month re-rating   (Today's date___/___/___)
(circle a number):

0	1	2	3	4	5	6
Not at all		Occasionally		Often		Any time

Goal 3: ....

....

....Today's date___/___/___

I can do this now (circle a number):

0	1	2	3	4	5	6
Not at all		Occasionally		Often		Any time

One month re-rating   (Today's date___/___/___)
(circle a number):

0	1	2	3	4	5	6
Not at all		Occasionally		Often		Any time

Two month re-rating   (Today's date___/___/___)
(circle a number):

0	1	2	3	4	5	6
Not at all		Occasionally		Often		Any time

Three month re-rating   (Today's date___/___/___)
(circle a number):

0	1	2	3	4	5	6
Not at all		Occasionally		Often		Any time

You have now thought about what life will be like if you make changes and set some goals. We hope you feel motivated to continue. In Section 2 we are going to help you understand what panic attacks are and what causes the experience of having panic attacks to turn into panic disorder.

UNDERSTANDING PANIC ATTACKS AND PANIC DISORDER

People who experience frequent panic attacks or panic disorder may often say to themselves, or ask themselves questions such as:

Am I going crazy?

Oh no, my heart's pounding again, what if I'm having a heart attack?

I'm really scared that when I get these physical sensations I may die.

If I go out will these physical sensations kick off again and will I pass out?

Should I give up things I find physically exerting?

In this section we will look at key information about panic attacks and panic disorder so you will feel better informed about why some people may have what can seem like overwhelming physical sensations in their body. We will then look at the ways in which panic attacks or panic disorder is affecting you. Panic attacks are sudden, and often unexplained, infrequent experiences of physical sensations. However, when these panic attacks become far more frequent and the person begins to anticipate and fear them, the experience of panic attacks can develop into what is known as panic disorder.

Understanding panic attacks or panic disorder is helped when they are viewed in terms of the way they make the person who experiences them physically feel, but also the type of thoughts the person has at the time, and what they do differently as a result. As covered in Section One, these three areas – physical feelings, thinking, changes in behaviour – can form a vicious panic cycle as one area begins to affect another.

Whilst the experience of panic will affect people in these three areas similarly, the impact upon people experiencing them may be different and individual, as from time to time everyone may experience overwhelming physical sensations in their body when they get anxious about something or stressed. But full panic disorder only develops in a much smaller number of people. Each person's

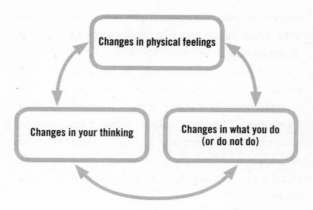

experience is therefore unique to them. So whilst this section will provide you with general information about panic attacks and panic disorder, it will also hopefully help you to understand your own personal experiences better. At the end of the section you will create your own vicious panic cycle, highlighting some of the changes you are experiencing in each of the areas above, to help you think about how they may be keeping your difficulties going round.

To help you understand your experience of panic better, we would like to introduce you to a few examples of people who have experienced panic attacks and panic disorder and how they have used the techniques covered in this book to help them feel better. Their situations may be different to yours but hopefully they will give you an inside view into the challenges people experiencing panic face and what they did about them.

Case studies

People who have used CBT self-help have said reading case studies of other people who have experienced panic is something they have found useful and encouraging. Two case studies are included in this self-help book:

Mike's story: Mike, a twenty-seven-year-old self-employed carpenter, began to get concerned when he started experiencing panic attacks. This caused him to begin to miss jobs, which was a significant problem for him and his family, as at that time his wife had taken time off as they had just had their second child. They were struggling to make ends meet.

Ria's story: Ria is a twenty-year-old personal assistant to a hospital consultant. Whilst struggling with mild anxiety most of her life, including the occasional panic attack, about a year ago she noticed herself experiencing panic attacks more and more frequently. She became increasingly concerned as to whether there was something physically wrong with her. Her GP gave her a clean bill of physical health, and she received a diagnosis of panic disorder.

Whilst the personal situations of Mike and Ria covered in these case studies will differ from your own, the techniques they have used are the same as the ones that may help you. Throughout the book we will return to the case studies to show you what their vicious panic cycles looked like, how they have put the techniques covered into action and to highlight what went well. Whilst the case studies show that using CBT self-help to manage their panic attacks or get on top of panic disorder was at times challenging, there were helpful things they did to overcome these challenges and keep going. It may not always be easy for you either, but being able to read through other people's experiences can help keep you on track. Let's meet Mike and Ria who have shared their stories and find out more about their situations.

Mike's Story

Mike was twenty-seven years of age with a job he loved as a carpenter. He also had a loving family, Sue his wife and two girls, three-year-old Sally and ten-month-old Martha. He had always felt in the very best of health and everything was going well for him and his family until eight months ago, when he started to experience overwhelming physical sensations for no obvious reason. These made him really scared and after a couple of times experiencing them he began to get a bit worried that something may be wrong with him and that he was going crazy. Initially he decided to carry on working to see if he could work through them, not least as he had just landed a long job renovating a block of flats and needed the steady income, especially now Martha was born and Sue had decided to leave work. He carried on working for another couple of months but started to miss the odd day at work after experiencing a few more episodes of having these overwhelming physical sensations, one of which was in the middle of the night, waking him up.

One day, when out with his family walking the dog through the fields at the back of his house, Mike was overcome with fear when he had these really bad physical sensations again. This time they scared him so much he said he did not want to walk through the fields again and avoided other busy places in case he had another attack. Sue insisted he see their GP, Dr Burkes.

Mike told Dr Burkes about these sudden, overwhelming physical sensations he was having about three or four times a month. They included being short of breath, having choking sensations and feeling dizzy. Mike also explained how, although it sounded silly, at times he started to feel as if he was de-tached from the world around him. Dr Burkes listened to Mike's chest and checked his blood pressure but said all seemed fine, so asked him a few wider questions about himself and any-thing troubling him. He found out that over the last few months Mike had began to feel a little unsettled at work, and he even felt a little stressed travelling to work now he had to drive over a high suspension bridge to get there, a route he had always previously avoided.

Dr Burke said that he felt Mike may be experiencing 'panic attacks' and whilst he did not know what was causing them, he thought they may partly be related to Mike's work. He also said that he may find reading a self-help book called *How to Beat Panic Disorder One Step at a Time* helpful. He said this book would give Mike more information about panic attacks and would help him make a Panic Diary to better understand some of the things that may be setting his physical sensa-tions off. Dr Burke also said that if they were related to anything in particular, the book would take him through a CBT intervention called Exposure Therapy to help him get on top of the physical sensations.

Mike was glad to hear there was nothing physically wrong with him, but was a little bit sceptical about how a self-help book could help. He also still had no idea about what could be setting the physical sensations off, and in particular what could set them off when he was asleep! After he started to read through the book however, he soon realised that CBT self-help was in fact widely recommended by the NHS because it really seemed to work. Mike also actually thought he might like this way of working as it put him in control. It might help him understand why he kept getting these scary physical sensations and enable him to get on top of them. You can find out what Mike learned after completing his Panic Diary and how he got on with Exposure Therapy in Section 5.

Ria's Story

Ria was getting along really nicely in her job as a personal assistant to Dr Bashan, a hospital consultant who specialised in diabetes but was soon to retire. Ria was twenty-years-old, had been in her job since leaving college two years before and really loved it, already being promoted several times. However, about four months ago she noticed herself beginning to experience 'panic attacks' more and more frequently and become increasingly worried that there may be something physically wrong with her.

At first she put these 'panic attacks' simply down to stress. She had always been a bit stressed and was well aware of how stress made her feel in her body. But these physical sensations seemed different. They were more intense and seemed to last longer. She remembered her first panic attack really well. She was just about to leave the office when, all of a sudden, she felt really hot, her heart raced, she started to shake, felt sick and became dizzy, so much so that she gripped her desk and sat down. She began to feel there might be something very seriously wrong with her and decided to start to look out for any physical signs that may indicate she was ill. After that she experienced 'panic attacks' more often, increasing her belief that something may seriously happen to her if she kept getting these physical sensations. She felt it might also help if she reduced physically exerting herself, so she gave up jogging and even started to walk less.

She made an appointment to see her GP, Dr White. He checked her blood pressure and even took some blood to run a blood test and made an appointment to see Ria when the blood results were back. The next few days were terrible; Ria began to experience 'panic attacks' more and more frequently over these days and became convinced that something was wrong, even that she may be dying. However, to her surprise, when seeing Dr White to discuss the blood results, Ria was relieved to learn that nothing was wrong but she struggled to believe it. She asked Dr White why else would she be getting these terrible physical sensations if nothing was wrong? Dr White then mentioned something called 'panic disorder' and suggested Ria went along to see Amanda, a Psychological Wellbeing Practitioner (or PWP for short), for an assessment. If she was experiencing panic disorder, Amanda could tell her more about what it was and could help her.

Two weeks later, Ria saw Amanda, who carried out an assessment. Amanda said that it did seem Ria was experiencing panic disorder and explained that when we become stressed our bodies release something called adrenaline. She explained how this is a perfectly natural process and could actually keep us safe. Ria knew this as she had been a worrier most of her life, but these physical sensations were different; they were much more frequent and lasted longer. Amanda said this was because when Ria had been stressed in the past, she was not worrying about the physical sensations and what they meant. However, this time she was also getting really anxious about the physical sensations so was always monitoring her body for signs of them and thinking they meant she was seriously ill or might even die.

Amanda then indicated how this kicked off a 'panic cycle' and how there was a link between getting these physical sensations, the thoughts going through Ria's head when she got them, and what she did as a result, increasing her anxiety levels more generally. Amanda then gave some good news, indicating that Cognitive Behaviour Therapy (CBT) self-help, supported by a self-help book on panic disorder, might be helpful. Using it she would better understand 'Panic Disorder'. She would complete a Panic Diary to give her an idea as to what may be kicking her panic attacks off and what may be keeping them going, leading to her panic attacks becoming panic disorder. Ria was relieved that there was something that might help, and especially that it was based on CBT. She had heard about CBT and its evidence base from the National Institute for Health and Clinical Evidence (NICE) through her job. You can find out how Ria completed her Panic Diary and what she learned about her Panic Disorder in Section 5.

Answering some questions you may have

Hopefully after reading the case studies you have begun to understand more about the ways in which people may experience panic attacks or panic disorder. You will hear more about what they did to better manage those unwanted physical sensations and the techniques they learned to get on top of them in Section 5. However, you are still likely to have a number of questions about why you are experiencing panic attacks or panic disorder and what you can do about them. Now we will try to answer some of the common questions people who experience panic often have.

Question 1: What are panic attacks?

People often report their panic attacks as being associated with the experience of a range of intense and unexpected physical sensations that cause intense fear but for which they cannot identify an obvious cause. These physical sensations can vary widely between people, however commonly reported ones include a combination of:

- Shortness of breath or feeling smothered

- Hot or cold flushes

- Chest pain or discomfort

- Numbness or tingling sensations

- Heart palpitations or racing heart

- Dizziness or lightheadedness

- Sensations of choking

- Sweating

- Shaking or trembling

- Tingling, tickling or burning sensation on the skin

- Feeling sick or an upset stomach

Once these physical sensations are experienced, some people also report experiencing a sense of unreality, as if they're detached from the world around them, with fears of 'losing control', 'going crazy' or even a fear of dying.

Panic attacks can be experienced anywhere and at any time and often people are unable to identify anything obvious that may trigger them. They can therefore be experienced in situations where there is no obvious threat or stress. Panic attacks can even occur when people are sleeping and wake them up. There also seems to be some relationship between panic attacks and major or stressful life events such as moving job, getting married, the death of a loved one or getting divorced. Most commonly however, they are experienced when people are away from home, usually lasting between five and twenty-five minutes, with longer ones often reaching their peak within ten minutes. Although when having a panic attack it may feel as though you are in serious trouble, panic attacks are not dangerous and should not cause any physical harm.

The NHS Choices website has excellent resources you can use to find out more about panic attacks. This includes an audio extract from Professor Chris Williams, a leading mental health expert in this area, who outlines the early warning signs and experience of panic attacks and what can be done about them. You can listen to it at the following link.

http://www.nhs.uk/conditions/stress-anxiety-depression/pages/understanding-panic-attacks.aspx www.

Question 2: What causes panic attacks?

The physical sensations associated with a panic attack are caused by your body going into an adrenalin response in response to something perceived as a harmful event or a threat to survival. In response to the perceived threat, the body produces adrenaline and in turn this causes several physical effects in the body. This is sometimes known as a 'fight' or 'flight' response. These include a faster beating heart, tensing of muscles or a quickening of breath as the body seeks to protect itself from the threat, either by running away, fighting or by freezing in an attempt to promote relaxation if either of these is impossible.

There is still a lot of expert debate about why our bodies go into this mode in response to threat and why this results in panic attacks with some people. Whilst the underlying cause of panic attacks is not clear, various theories have proposed that they may have an evolutionary basis, be caused by our genetics or result from the way we perceive physical sensations in the body, events or situations as threatening that otherwise do not have any objective threat or danger.

The way our bodies have evolved: Some experts argue that evolution has primed us and other animals to become fearful of situations that could pose a potential threat to our survival. For example, in primitive times being in open spaces could have left our ancestors vulnerable to attack from predators, whilst enclosed spaces could have made escape difficult. Therefore having an inbuilt predisposition to become panicky would have made our ancestors more likely to avoid them. Or it may have helped to keep them safe by preparing the body for immediate action and therefore help secure the survival of the species. Although we generally no longer face the same type of threats in modern society, as a result of the way our bodies have evolved, on some occasions our bodies may still respond in similar ways.

Perception of events or situations: Sometimes panic attacks may be set off by the way people overestimate the amount of risk that a common, everyday situation, event or physical symptom presents. People may have thoughts about the physical sensations of panic in their body like 'I'm having a heart attack', 'I'm going to faint' or even 'I'm going to die'. When a person responds inappropriately to a perceived threat causing the body to go into an adrenaline response, this suggests their response has been caused by the way they perceive their physical sensations, events or situations.

Our genetic makeup: A large number of studies have been carried out involving families or twins to try to identify a potential genetic basis to panic disorder. Researchers have identified several chemicals in the brain that in some people may make them oversensitive to stressful situations, whereby their bodies release adrenaline, frequently kicking off the adrenalin response to otherwise neutral events or situations with no obvious threat or danger. Another line of research proposes that some people's brains may be oversensitive to carbon dioxide, triggering physical sensations such as suffocation and the potential panic cycle.

Use of drugs or stimulants: Sometimes panic-like physical symptoms have been identified following people's use of a range of non-prescribed stimulants such as mind-altering drugs. These include cocaine or amphetamines. They have also been associated with the use of some medications, especially on occasions when it has been stopped abruptly, not used as prescribed or not under the direction of a medical professional. Even having large amounts of caffeinated drinks such as energy drinks, tea or coffee (especially filter coffee) has been associated with panic attacks in some people.

Medical reasons: Whilst panic has many possible causes which can also work in combination, there are a small number of medical conditions that can increase the risk of people experiencing the range of intense and unexpected physical sensations discussed in Question 1. Most commonly these include having:

- An overactive thyroid gland (called hyperthyroidism)

- Low blood sugar (called hypoglycaemia)

- A minor heart problem that occurs when one of the heart's valves doesn't close correctly (called a mitral valve prolapse)

If you are experiencing panic attacks or panic disorder then it may be good to see your GP to rule out the possibility that you are experiencing any of these.

Question 3: What is the difference between panic attacks and panic disorder?

So far in answer to Questions 1 and 2 we have only

discussed 'panic attacks'. But there is also something called 'panic disorder', which is similar, but not the same thing. Both involve those intense and unexpected physical sensations described in response to Question 1, but having panic attacks does not mean you have panic disorder. The experience of panic attacks can also be commonly experienced across a range of other anxiety disorders. For example, people who fear spiders will experience a range of physical sensations when they see, talk or think about spiders, but they will be aware that they are related to their arachnophobia. They therefore do not explicitly fear the specific physical sensations themselves, although they may still find them unpleasant. However, with panic attacks (and more generally, panic disorder), the physical sensations themselves become the source of the fear.

As discussed in Question 2, many people experience panic attacks for a variety of reasons and although they can be highly distressing, there is little reason to worry if they are experienced occasionally. However, some people who experience panic attacks go on to develop panic disorder. Unlike the experience of the occasional panic attack, panic disorder is associated with frequent and repeated panic attacks combined with significant changes in behaviour and increased concern about having further attacks. Given the frequency of the panic attacks, the person may become so distressed when they experience the overwhelming physical sensations that they begin to think things like they may be going to collapse or faint, go crazy, lose control or even die. Having such thoughts can then in themselves cause the body to release further adrenaline and it goes into 'flight, fight or freeze' mode, continuing and increasing the experience of the 'vicious cycle of panic'. Given the increased frequency and significant impact on the lives of people experiencing panic disorder, it is a mental health diagnosis that people may receive from a health or mental health professional.

Question 4: Why me?

As we have already discussed, everyone experiences the physical sensations that are set off when our body goes into an adrenalin response and as such your experience of these physical sensations is not unusual. As has been discussed in Question 2, there are several competing theories as to why people experience panic attacks or go on to develop panic disorder and there is always the possibility that your own experience may be caused by a combination of these factors. However, whilst there is likely no simple explanation as to why you are experiencing panic attacks or panic disorder, we know they can affect people from any walk of life and any age. Although they most commonly begin between the ages of 15 and 25, with half of the people who develop panic disorder doing so before the age of 24.

In their lifetime, about 1 in 4 people will have consulted a health or medical professional for 'panic attacks', falling to about 1 in 25 people who will have been diagnosed with panic disorder and about 1 in 100 diagnosed with panic disorder that has also developed into something else called agoraphobia. Agoraphobia is a fear of open spaces that develops when people associate specific places, for example the bus or shopping centre, with the thing setting off their physical sensations. Over time they begin to avoid these situations, only leaving the house with a partner or friend, or in the most extreme cases being unwilling to leave the house altogether. What is clear is that once someone starts to experience frequent panic attacks or panic disorder, they report noticing changes to their physical wellbeing, their thinking and what they do as a result. These are the things we can do something about using this CBT self-help approach. In some ways it doesn't matter how you ended up here. What matters is breaking into your vicious panic cycle. Your hard work in reading and engaging with activities in this book will help you work towards the goals you have already set in Section 1 and get on top of your panic.

Question 5: Why does having panic attacks or panic disorder feel like it's taken over my whole life?

People who experience frequent panic attacks or panic disorder often report their life as being affected in three main areas:

1. *Changes in how they feel physically:* This is the area that causes most initial concern as people begin to become concerned about the intense and unexpected onset of physical sensations for which they cannot identify an obvious cause and lead them to experience intense fear.

2. *Changes in their behaviour:* People may begin to actively monitor their bodies for signs that these physical sensations are returning and begin to anticipate and fear their onset. Some people may even start doing things like avoiding activities or places they feel may be associated with the onset of their physical sensations and may find themselves leaving the house less and less.

3. *Changes to their thinking:* In response to the

physical panic sensations, unhelpful or cata-
strophic thoughts may run through the person's
mind, such that they may think they are going
to collapse, lose control, that they are going
crazy, or may think their life is at risk as a result.
For example, chest pains could be interpreted
as a heart attack.

One thing leads to another and these three areas
each have a knock-on effect on the other, creating
the vicious cycle of panic. In the case of panic disorder these areas can get into a state of prolonged
activation creating the vicious panic cycle fuelled
by the release of adrenaline into the body, further
stoking and maintaining the panic cycle. This can
make it feel to the person as if panic attacks or panic
disorder are taking over their whole life, causing
them to live in a state of fear.

The vicious panic cycles of Mike and Ria, whose
case studies you have already been introduced to,
are presented over. The specific details may be different to your experience of how panic is affecting
you in the three areas described above. However,
it is likely you can relate to at least parts of each
vicious panic cycle. Additionally, considering the
similarities and differences between both examples may help you to further appreciate the difference between panic attacks, as demonstrated in

Mike's example, and panic disorder, as experienced by Ria.

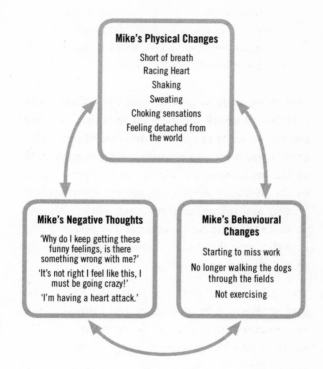

Mike's Physical Changes

Short of breath
Racing Heart
Shaking
Sweating
Choking sensations
Feeling detached from the world

Mike's Negative Thoughts

'Why do I keep getting these funny feelings, is there something wrong with me?'
'It's not right I feel like this, I must be going crazy!'
'I'm having a heart attack.'

Mike's Behavioural Changes

Starting to miss work
No longer walking the dogs through the fields
Not exercising

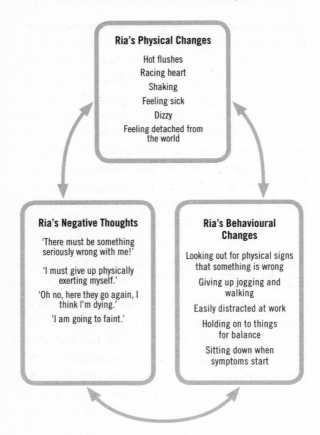

Ria's Physical Changes

Hot flushes

Racing heart

Shaking

Feeling sick

Dizzy

Feeling detached from
the world

Ria's Negative Thoughts

'There must be something
seriously wrong with me!'

'I must give up physically
exerting myself.'

'Oh no, here they go again, I
think I'm dying.'

'I am going to faint.'

**Ria's Behavioural
Changes**

Looking out for physical signs
that something is wrong

Giving up jogging and
walking

Easily distracted at work

Holding on to things
for balance

Sitting down when
symptoms start

Panic attacks or panic disorder therefore impact
upon all three of these areas with changes in one
area affecting another, leading to the vicious panic
cycle. For example, in Mike's 'Vicious Panic Cycle',

his experience of the onset of intense and unexpected physical sensations led him to have negative thoughts about the meaning and potential causes of these sensations and to him avoiding activities such as going to work and walking the dogs. In response to her intense and unexpected physical sensations, Ria's 'Vicious Panic Cycle' concerning her panic disorder saw her having several unhelpful thoughts about the meaning of these sensations, even leading her to have an extremely distressing and extreme thought – 'I am going to faint.' In response to these things, she actively began to continually monitor physical changes in her body and give up on physical activities like jogging. She became increasingly fearful of having another panic attack.

By comparing both of these vicious panic cycles, factors that may lead to the experience of panic attacks turning into panic disorder can be better understood. Unlike Mike, in response to her unexpected physical sensations, Ria's vicious panic cycle highlights how she became increasingly fearful concerning the onset of further physical sensations and began to continually monitor her body to check for physical sensations. She gave up jogging and walking long distances because they caused physical exertion. Increased levels of fear maintained her unwanted physical sensations by releasing further adrenaline and thereby triggering the 'flight, fight or freeze' response. This leads to the vicious panic cycle being activated again and becoming increasingly more difficult to break out of. Furthermore, the negative effects can spill over and cause problems in other areas of life. For example, in Mike's case study he started to miss work, at a time when money was short whereas Ria became more easily distracted at work.

Question 6: What can be done about panic attacks or panic disorder?

The good news is that there are a number of things that can be done about panic attacks and panic disorder. The National Institute for Health and Care Excellence (NICE), the organisation that recommends treatments for the National Health Service, has published guidelines for members of the public (https://www.nice.org.uk/guidance/cg113/ifp/chapter/panic-disorder). www. These provide further information on panic and overview the range of 'evidence-based treatments', some of which are presented below. These are treatments that have been researched extensively and are known to work for many people who use them. There is also further information for family or carers of people with panic disorder that also includes some useful help and advice to understand panic and discover potential ways to help (http://www.nice.org.uk/guidance/cg113/ifp/ chapter/Information-for-families-and-carers-of-people-with-panic-disorder [www.]).

CBT Self-Help (or sometimes called bibliotherapy): This is an example of the way you are working here. The approach is based on Cognitive Behavioural Therapy, a psychological therapy that lends itself readily to a self-help format. CBT self-help consists of the same content and techniques you would engage in if having face-to-face therapy with a therapist. The approach can be used without any support from a trained health professional, but having support can be really effective, especially when people really find themselves struggling with motivation or concentration. Many people use this type of approach with the support of their GP, nurse or (if in England) a Psychological Wellbeing Practitioner (PWP). If you think you would benefit from support to use this approach, you can ask your GP about what is available in your area. If in England you can find it here and self-refer: http://www.iapt.nhs.uk/services/. [www.] If you are using the self-help book on your own, you are still advised to consult your primary health care professional regularly, to keep them updated on your progress.

Psychological Therapies: To many this represents the most well known way of working to overcome emotional difficulties such as those experienced with panic. People attend regular sessions with a trained therapist who will provide the treatment to help them overcome their emotional difficulty. If interested in this form of support, however, you should check with your GP as to the length of the waiting list. Whilst NICE may recommend a range of psychological therapies for other emotional difficulties, CBT treatment is the only psychological therapy recommended for panic disorder. As with the use of CBT self-help, if receiving psychological therapy you are still advised to see your GP or primary healthcare professional regularly to assess progress.

Medication: As well as CBT being available to help you get on top of your panic, medication is also an available option. If you decide medication may be the best option for you, then first of all make an appointment to see your healthcare professional. They will discuss whether medication is suitable for you, how it will work and any unwanted effects that you may experience if you took the medication prescribed. If you decide to take the medication, your healthcare professional will point out that whilst the medication is not addictive like cigarettes, if you stop taking it, miss or reduce a dose, you may experience some unpleasant symptoms called discontinuation symptoms and that if you do you should make a further appointment. Whilst discontinuation symptoms can be experienced across a range of medication, understanding the impact they can have on someone seeking help for panic disorder is especially important. This is because they could have the potential to set off the vicious panic cycle once again, if you did not fully understand the cause of the physical symptoms. It is therefore important that you do not stop taking any medication without first discussing your plans with your GP. Furthermore, if you start taking medication for your panic disorder, you should arrange to see your healthcare professional at 2, 4, 6 and 12 weeks after starting the treatment. This will enable you to decide whether to continue or consider another treatment.

If you decide medication is your preferred option for panic disorder and your healthcare professional thinks it is suitable for you, then NICE recommends a selective serotonin reuptake inhibitor (often shortened to SSRI). This is a type of antidepressant, but one that has been specifically approved for the treatment of panic disorder. You can find more information about SSRIs on the NHS Choices website:

http://www.nhs.uk/conditions/ssris-(selective-
serotonin-reuptake-inhibitors)/Pages/
Introduction.aspx www.

If an SSRI is not suitable for you, then your healthcare provider may suggest a medication called imipramine or clomipramine. Although these medications are not yet licensed for use in the treatment of panic disorder, they have been shown to be effective and are recommended by NICE. NICE does not however recommend an antipsychotic, a sedative antihistamine or a benzodiazepine for the treatment of panic disorder.

Question 7: Will it happen again?

The good news is that about 70% of people who had been diagnosed with panic disorder and received treatment were still managing to keep on top of their panic disorder when followed up eight years after being diagnosed. That means however that about 30% of people go on to experience panic disorder again. Unfortunately, there is currently no agreed way of knowing who will go on to experience panic disorder again in the future and who will not. However, what we know is that people who learn techniques to identify warning signs that their panic disorder may be returning can put those techniques that worked for them before into practice to stop their panic getting a grip again. Developing panic disorder is, however, very different to having an isolated and infrequent panic attack. As has been discussed, everyone experiences the occasional physical symptoms associated with the 'flight, fight or freeze' response, indeed they may keep you safe. So helping to distinguish between a panic attack and the potential return of panic disorder can also go some way to stopping panic disorder from returning or indeed from developing.

In Section 4, you will also learn how to create a *Panic Disorder Relapse Prevention Toolkit*. Developing this Toolkit means that should you begin to have unexpected and frequent panic attacks again, you know what action to take before they begin to trigger the vicious panic cycle. This will help ensure that the panic attacks do not develop into or cause a resurgence of panic disorder. Unfortunately, we cannot guarantee that someone will not experience panic disorder again in the future. What we can guarantee though is that the tools learned in this book will better equip them to get on top of their panic attacks or get over panic disorder. The tools and techniques you will learn in this self-help book are lifelong skills to help keep on top of your panic attacks or panic disorder. Rather than trying to avoid experiencing panic attacks again, it is more helpful to look out for the early warning signs that first showed you (or people who care about you) that you were experiencing panic disorder and to take action if you need to. Hopefully now you have read this section you have realised that by taking actions to avoid experiencing those unexpected physical sensations (such as always actively looking out for them or avoiding exerting yourself) you increase your fear that the physical sensations associated with a panic attack may return – making them more likely to return!

How is panic affecting you?

Now you have thought about how panic attacks affect us physically, our thoughts and what we do (or not do) as a result and you better appreciate the things that turn the experience of panic attacks into panic disorder, it is time to apply this new understanding to your own situation. Just like the examples of Mike's and Ria's Vicious Panic Cycles above, write into each of the three areas on the diagram over to create your own Vicious Panic Cycle.

Think about the unexpected physical sensations you experience associated with your panic and write these in the 'Physical' box. Next, think about what you do more of, or have stopped doing, when you experience these physical sensations and write these in the 'Behaviours' box. Finally, in the 'Thoughts' box write examples of thoughts you have when experiencing the physical symptoms. Try to express these thoughts in a way that is as close as possible to the way you would express the thoughts verbally to yourself, or if the thought is an image try to describe it as best you can.

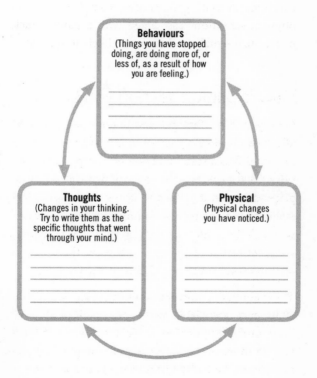

Behaviours
(Things you have stopped doing, are doing more of, or less of, as a result of how you are feeling.)

Thoughts
(Changes in your thinking. Try to write them as the specific thoughts that went through your mind.)

Physical
(Physical changes you have noticed.)

All of these areas interact and result in a vicious panic cycle that is associated with your experience of panic attacks or related to your panic disorder. Each area has a knock-on effect on what is happening in the other areas and they all impact upon each other. Or in the case of panic disorder, each area helps to maintain the panic attacks. However, the good news is that breaking into this panic cycle in any one of the areas will help to reverse the cycle and help you get on top of your panic. Just as it took time to establish a panic cycle, it will take time to reverse it the other way. But this self-help book, along with anyone supporting you, is here to show you the steps you can take to get on top of your panic.

The biggest step is acknowledging that things are not the way you want them to be and understanding more about panic attacks and how these can develop into panic disorder. Hopefully you are well on the way to doing this and it is now time to move onto Section 3. Here you will look at two key ways you can break the vicious panic cycle and begin to take the steps required to get on top of your panic.

Section 3

GETTING ON TOP OF PANIC THROUGH EXPOSURE TECHNIQUES

Well done on getting this far, we're really pleased you have stayed with the book. You have hopefully read some information about panic attacks and panic disorder and found this useful. For example, things such as how common they can be, what may cause them and the availability of treatments that can help. Now it's time to introduce you to some techniques so you can help break your own 'panic cycle' and get on top of your panic.

Key point:

The benefit of going through these techniques is to help you get on of your panic attacks or panic disorder. So if you're not sure about anything covered in Sections 1 or

2, go back over them at a time that suits you. You may find it helpful to fold the corner of pages, highlighting any key parts you feel you need to go back over. Don't be afraid of writing in the book or making notes, that is what it's for!

What is Exposure?

Exposure is a technique that helps people face things they fear. Research supports its use as a technique to help people get on top of their panic attacks or overcome their panic disorder. It is commonly used within a CBT approach.

As discussed in Section 2, given that you actually fear getting the physical sensations that Exposure will help you experience, it may be that just the thought of using Exposure will make you anxious. In fact, the thought itself may even be enough to kick those feelings of panic off! Even if the thought of doing exposure is enough to kick off your panic cycle, we still suggest you practise the techniques, to really help challenge your belief that your experience of the physical sensations must be related to something being wrong with you. This will help your body to learn that it does not need to react in that way.

Key features of Exposure techniques

Helps people identify the types of things or situations that kick off the feared physical sensations

Provides a structured approach that helps people face the objects or situations they fear, but doing so in a way that puts them in control

Grades the feared situations or objects from least to most fear, to help people begin to face them, but in a way they feel they can manage

Enables people to experience the key physical sensations they fear that kick off their 'panic cycle'

As fear of any specific object or situation begins to decrease, Exposure helps people to work up the list of things causing fear. In turn, this helps them challenge their belief that unexpected and intense physical symptoms mean there is something wrong with them

Over time, and with repeated experience of the feared physical sensations, the belief that these sensations mean there is anything physically wrong reduces, which reduces the fear of the physical sensations, breaking the 'panic cycle'.

How does Exposure work?

The relationship between fear and avoidance

As discussed in Section 2, when we fear something, our bodies produce a hormone called adrenaline into our system and this causes us to experience physical sensations. Over time, however, many people learn that one way to reduce their fear level and stop those unwanted physical sensations is to avoid the situations or objects that cause them to feel that way in the first place. As can be seen below, over time their fear drops.

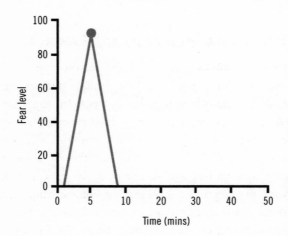

Effect of avoidance on level of fear

Avoiding the feared situations or objects therefore begins to provide some relief from the unwanted and intense physical sensations. In the longer term this relief from the 'panicky' physical sensations encourages people to keep avoiding the feared situations or objects triggering the panic, and avoidance leads to more avoidance. Over time a pattern of avoidance becomes established. Although this may represent a solution in the short term, whenever the situations or objects causing fear cannot be avoided and need to be faced, the panicky physical sensations kick off again and result in experiencing that fear about fear, and the 'panic cycle' begins again. So avoidance may be helpful in the short term but just maintains the problem in the longer term.

Breaking the relationship with Exposure

Exposure works by providing the person experiencing the 'panic cycle' with a technique supporting them to gradually expose themselves to the situation or object causing them fear without avoiding it and escaping from it. It does so in a way that is under their control, starting with the situations or objects causing least fear and encouraging them to remain with the physical sensations for long enough for those physical sensations to reduce naturally, without avoiding or escaping from them. Staying with the fearful situation or object until the physical sensations come down on their own is called 'habituation'. With 'habituation' experienced a number of times, the person learns that the physical sensations representing their 'alarm reaction' will actually disappear on their own if they stay long enough in the situation. Also, as can be seen below, when the Exposure exercise is repeated, the maximum level of fear it causes begins to reduce and habituation is reached in a shorter amount of time.

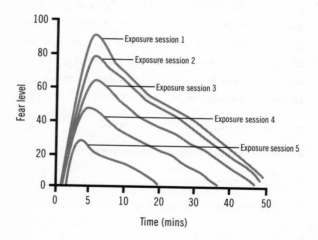

Overcoming Fear Through Exposure

Eventually, with repeated exposure, the 'alarm reaction' gets turned off, breaking the link between the situation and the object and the experience of the physical sensations, in turn stopping the 'panic cycle'. Over time also, the body begins to get used to the once-feared physical sensations and the 'fear of fear' that once maintained the panic attacks leading to panic disorder reduces.

How can Exposure work to break the panic cycle?

You have come across the Panic Cycle already in Section 2 and we discussed how the stress-related physical sensations are the body's 'alarm reaction' on occasions letting you know, or making you believe, that you may need to do something to stay safe. You've also learned that a number of things can set the 'alarm reaction' off, such as:

- The way our bodies have evolved

- Perception of events or situations

- Our genetic makeup

- Use of drugs or stimulants

- Medical reasons

We have also suggested that people who experience frequent 'panic attacks' and begin to struggle with 'panic disorder' have, over time, developed a belief that these sensations mean there is something wrong with them, to the extent that they actually begin to 'fear the fear' of having them. They may have also become increasingly sensitive to them, noticing even small changes in the physical sensations in their body. Just having this fear also ends up increasing the likelihood of the person experiencing another 'panic attack', and the panic cycle begins again, possibly turning into panic disorder, a real 'Catch 22'.

Exposure enables you to recognise the situations or objects you fear that cause you to experience the stress-related physical sensations. It then provides you with a structured approach to expose yourself to those situations or objects. But it does so in a way that's under your control. The more you experience these intense and unexpected physical symptoms, the more you begin to get over the fear they cause:

- Your body becoming more comfortable with, or better able to tolerate, the physical sensations, such that they no longer always trigger the 'alarm reaction'

- Helping you recognise the link between the objects or situations causing fear and the physical symptoms they cause your body to experience

- Learning that these physical sensations are triggered by a number of different things, over time reducing your fear of them and thereby helping you to challenge your belief that they mean something is physically wrong with you

Over time your body will get used to the physical sensations you experience. This will help to reduce the link between your experience of these physical sensations and your fear that there is something physically wrong with you. You will also begin to become less alert to them. In time this will slowly reduce the number of panic cycles you have been experiencing.

> **Remember:** At times, you will still experience the physical sensations associated with stress. Everyone does and, on occasions, these may help to keep you safe. But you will hopefully no longer jump to the conclusion that these mean there is something physically wrong with you. This will help break the 'panic cycle' as highlighted overleaf.

When people become stressed their body releases adrenaline, setting off the body's 'alarm reaction'.

The person feels the physical sensations of this alarm reaction and thinks something must be physically wrong with them, which in turn releases more adrenaline and continues the alarm reaction that maintains the physical sensations.

Panic attacks become less frequent and less intense.

Over time the body is increasingly able to tolerate the physical feelings it experiences, helping the person challenge their belief that stress-related physical sensations mean there is something physically wrong, breaking their fear of fear.

Similar repeated experiences are taken as further 'evidence' that something physical must be wrong, increasing the person's belief that something *is* wrong.

Exposure enables people to face the situation or object they are afraid of, experiencing the physical sensations they fear but in a way that's under their control.

As they now increasingly fear the physical sensations, they begin to look out for signs of these physical changes in the body, making them increasingly alert to them.

Using Exposure to Break the Panic Cycle

In a moment you are going to make an Exposure Plan to help you get on top of your 'panic attacks' or beat your panic disorder. But first you need to understand the rules of Exposure.

The rules of Exposure

When making your Exposure Plan, you should pay attention to four rules that will help guide you and ensure that Exposure is most likely to work for you. These four rules are described below, and then returned to when discussing the steps to take when making an Exposure Plan.

Rule 1: Graded

To help you engage with Exposure, once you recognise the things that 'set your alarm reaction off' it's important to grade these in terms of how much fear they cause you. You then rank these from 'least' to 'most' fear, to create a 'fear hierarchy'. Once you have graded your hierarchy, as your first Exposure exercise you should select the situation or object that causes you at least 50% fear. Choosing a situation or object causing you at least 50% fear hopefully ensures:

1). It is at a low enough level for you to feel you can engage in Exposure.

2). But is high enough to enable you to notice that with Exposure your body will naturally become more comfortable with the physical symptoms that have been triggered and they will subside.

Once the physical sensations subside, the idea is that you then repeat Exposure. However this time you start with the next situation or object in your hierarchy that was originally rated as causing a little more fear.

> **IMPORTANT:** Choosing an object or situation causing at least 50% fear to start Exposure is advisable. However, if you feel this is simply too much fear to get started with, then think about starting with an object or situation causing slightly less fear. If possible, it's good not to go too low. We recommend at least 40–50% is required or else habituation cannot take place.

Rule 2: Without distraction

Rule 2 encourages you to do each Exposure exercise without being distracted by other things or people. It's understandable you may want to rely on things that help distract you, if that distraction is helping you manage your fear. For example, people may report that being with other people helps them to walk to the shops when they would struggle to go on their own, or listening to music helps them to go shopping. However, for Exposure to work you really need to face the situation or object causing you fear 'head on', without being distracted. This enables you and your body to get used to the physical sensations without having to be dependent on things that distract you. If you are dependent on these things then when they are not there, you will find yourself back at the beginning with regard to the amount of fear an object or situation causes. The ideal is therefore that you do each Exposure exercise without any form of distraction. However, if this would cause too much fear to begin with, it's OK to start an Exposure exercise with distraction, but try to drop it later. Ensure your hierarchy steps include the element you add and subtract.

IMPORTANT: Ideally you should plan to do each Exposure exercise without any form of distraction. But if this is not possible with any specific Exposure exercise, initially plan to do the exercise with the distraction but then plan to drop it with another Exposure exercise. It's better to get started with an Exposure exercise with distraction helping you, than not start at all.

Rule 3: Prolonged

The next rule relates to how long you should expose yourself to the situation or object for. It is *very important* to be aware that you should not expose yourself to the object or situation for a pre-determined length of time. If you do this it could result in you stopping the exercise before your adrenaline has been used up and before those unwanted physical sensations have reduced. Therefore you should always expose yourself to the object or situation for as long as it takes your fear to drop by 50% from what you recorded it as at the start of the Exposure exercise. Everyone is different and no one knows how long it will take for your physical symptoms to reduce by this amount. So it may be helpful to put aside 90 minutes for your Exposure exercise initially, but then reduce the time once you get an idea of how long each Exposure exercise is taking for each step of the hierarchy.

IMPORTANT: Do not grade your Exposure exercises by time, but continue each Exposure exercise until your fear has dropped by 50% from that recorded at the start of the exercise.

Rule 4: Repeated

Repeatedly expose yourself to the situation or object you are working on as your Exposure exercise for as many times as it takes until your fear rating stops rising quickly when preparing to do the exercise and does not go beyond what you consider to be a manageable level at the start of the exercise. This will vary from person to person, but many people report that having 30–40% fear of an object or situation can be managed, and that this level often just goes when they are distracted by doing something else. Try to repeat each Exposure exercise as many times as you need to each week, until you find the fear manageable. Remember, repeating the Exposure exercises can be tiring, but the more you do each exercise, the more likely there will be benefits. Many people reported that doing each Exposure exercise 4–5 times a week was really beneficial. But this will vary from person to person given other competing demands in their lives that may get in the way. Therefore, try to aim to complete Exposure exercises about 4–5 times a week when you can and if you achieve it, that's great. If not, just do your best!

> **IMPORTANT:** Repeat each Exposure exercise for as many times as it takes for the fear associated with each Exposure exercise to become more manageable.

The four steps to make an Exposure Plan

Step 1: Completing a Panic Diary

To help you 'get on top' of your panic attacks or panic disorder, in Step 1 you are asked to keep a record, 'My Panic Diary', for the next few days. This will help you get to 'know your enemy' better, and start you on the road to beating it. The first column asks you to record the situations or objects that set your 'alarm reaction' off. Remember from Section 2, at times you may find your 'alarm reaction' just going off without any obvious situation or object that seems to have triggered it. In these instances just write down what you were doing, then in the second column write down the specific details. The third column then asks you to identify the thought that was going through your head *just before* you noticed your physical sensations kick off. Remember, it is possible that your physical sensations have just started and there is no obvious thought, as would be the case where the intense physical sensations have an evolutionary cause.

If this is the case, that's fine just write 'none' in the third column.

In the next column, write down the physical sensations you have experienced as arising from the situation or object causing fear and that you associate with your panic attack. The range of common physical sensations that people associate with their panic attacks or panic disorder have been discussed in Section 2. Reminding yourself of these may help you better identify the type of physical sensations you experience. Once you have written the main physical sensations you experience down, rate them in terms of their intensity between 0 No Intensity, 50 Moderate Intensity and 100 Worst Intensity Ever. Next, identify what you fear so much about the physical sensations you experienced, for example what do you think will happen to you? Finally, look back over the row you have just completed and ask yourself what you have noticed about the object or situation you were in that set your intense physical sensations or panic off. For example, maybe you notice that they are often set off when you are alone, or in wide-open spaces, in work situations, or thinking about going to the park.

My Panic Diary

Situation or object causing fear	Where were you, when was this, who were you with?	What was the thought (if there was one) about the situation or object going through your head *just before* you noticed your physical sensations?	Physical sensations associated with panic	Intensity of these physical sensations (0–100)	What do you fear about these physical sensations (what do you think will happen)?	Have you noticed anything about the situation or object That may have set your physical sensations and panic off?

Intensity of Physical Symptoms Rating Scale

0	10	20	30	40	50	60	70	80	90	100
No Intensity					Moderate Intensity					Worst ever Intensity

Step 2: Identifying and rating things that set off your physical sensations

Look back over your Panic Diary and identify the situations or objects you have identified as kicking your physical sensations off. Write these in the **Things that set off my physical sensations** worksheet. Now, one by one, use the Fear Rating Scale at the bottom of the worksheet to rate each one in terms of how much fear they cause you to experience, between 0 which relates to 'No Fear at All' and 100 which equals 'Worst Fear Ever'.

Things that set off my physical sensations

Situation or Object Causing Fear	Fear Rating (0–100)

Fear Rating

0	25	50	75	100
No Fear	Mild Fear	Moderate Fear	Severe Fear	Full Panic

Things that set off my physical sensations

Situation or Object Causing Fear	Fear Rating (0–100)

Fear Rating				
0	25	50	75	100
No Fear	Mild Fear	Moderate Fear	Severe Fear	Full Panic

Step 3: Creating your 'Panic Cycle Ladder'

Now look at what you have written in the **Things that set off my physical sensations** worksheet and write these into the **Panic Cycle Ladder** worksheet. For every object or situation listed that causes *at least* 40% 'Moderate Fear', write this and the Fear Rating in the **Panic Cycle Ladder**. Write these situations or objects in the order reflecting their increased fear rating. So at the bottom write in the situation or object causing 'Least Fear' (but at least 50%) then write the situations or objects increasing in fear until finally you write the situation or object causing 'Most Fear' at the top of the ladder.

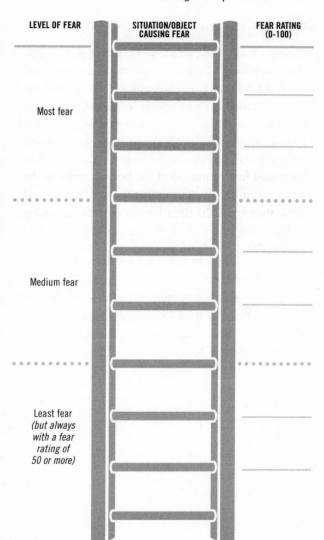

LEVEL OF FEAR

Most fear

Medium fear

Least fear
*(but always
with a fear
rating of
50 or more)*

SITUATION/OBJECT
CAUSING FEAR

FEAR RATING
(0-100)

Step 4: Facing your fears

Finally, you're going to use all the hard work you've done in Steps 1–3 to create an 'Exposure exercise'. This will inform how you're going to 'Face your Fears' but in a way that you're in control of and at a speed acceptable to you. To do this you should follow the Four Rules of Exposure discussed on page 72 to inform your Exposure plan.

First, identify a situation or object towards the bottom of your Panic Cycle Ladder, namely something that causes you at least 40–50% fear. It will most likely be around 50% fear, unless this is just too much for you to make a start, in which case it may be a little less (Exposure rule 1: *Graded*). Now plan an Exposure exercise based on this situation or object, paying attention to Exposure rule 2: *Without distraction*, and write this into the **Facing Your Fears** worksheet.

Now plan the date and time you're going to do your Exposure exercise, making sure you set enough time aside to do it. Remember you should plan for a long enough period of time (suggested as 90 minutes initially) for your fear to drop by 50% from that recorded at the start of the exercise (Exposure rule 3: *Prolonged*). Now it's time to actually do your Exposure exercise. It is really important for you to start to rate your fear using the 0–100 Fear Rating Scale at the bottom of the **Facing Your Fears** worksheet.

Rate your Fear using the Fear Rating Scale:

- When you are preparing for the Exposure exercise.

- Immediately before the start of the Exposure exercise.

- When you feel that your fear has fallen by 50% from your rating at the start of the Exposure exercise.

If it has fallen by 50%:

- Write the fear rating in the End of Exercise column and record the time you have completed the Exposure exercise in the final Duration column.

- Repeat this Exposure exercise until you feel it's more manageable (Exposure rule 4: Repeated).

Facing Your Fears Worksheet

Exposure exercise

Date and time you will do your next Exposure exercise		Exposure fear ratings (0–100)			
		Preparing for Exposure exercise	Start of Exposure exercise	End of Exposure exercise	Duration of Exposure exercise
	Session 1				
	Session 2				

	0	25	50	75	100
Fear Rating	No Fear	Mild Fear	Moderate Fear	Severe Fear	Full Panic

Session 3					
Session 4					
Session 5					
Session 6					

Comments

- You are now ready to choose the next Exposure exercise for a situation or object rated with a little more fear (Exposure rule 1: Graded) from your Panic Cycle Ladder and then repeat Step 4 using a new **Facing Your Fears** worksheet.

If, however, it has not fallen by 50%:

- Set another date and time to do the Exposure exercise again; the sooner you can have another go the better.

- Then repeat the exercise until the fear rating has fallen by 50% (Exposure rule 3: *Prolonged*) for as many times it takes for you to feel that the fear caused by the exposure exercise is now manageable (Exposure rule 4: *Repeated*).

- You are then ready to choose the next Exposure exercise for a situation or object rated with a little more fear from your Panic Cycle Ladder and then repeat Step 4 on a new **Facing Your Fears** worksheet.

How long should you continue with Exposure to get on top of your panic cycle?

Using a new **Facing Your Fears** worksheet, continue Steps 1 to 4 to help you move up your Exposure hierarchy. Repeat this until you have successfully reduced your fear to a manageable level for all the situations or objects you have listed in your Panic Cycle Ladder or until you have reached the goals you set yourself in Chapter 1. Hopefully getting over your fear of these situations or objects has also helped you challenge your belief that having physical sensations associated with fear means there is something physically wrong with you. In turn this will help you become less alert to your physical sensations.

Remember: always use the Rules of Exposure when planning and completing your Exposure plan and continue to complete the worksheets. Many people report that this really helps them.

If you've successfully used Exposure to get on top of the things that cause you panic then great stuff and well done! Now move on to the next section, that will help you develop a Relapse Prevention Toolkit to enable you to keep on top of your panic attacks or panic disorder.

THE RELAPSE PREVENTION TOOLKIT

This final section is for people who have already read the previous sections and completed the activities. If you're reading this section after completing the previous ones, congratulations are in order. It means you've almost completed your plan to get on top of your panic and are hopefully feeling better, and likely making progress towards the goals you set at the start. You will have committed time and hard work putting the techniques and skills you have learned into your daily life to get here. It's only through the things you've done using this book that this has happened. You have successfully helped yourself to feel better.

The final step is to keep the progress going and think about staying well and dealing with any difficulties you may face in the future. Therefore we would really encourage you to take this final step by working through this section. For many people, this moment can be a really positive sign that things have improved. But it's understandably a time where you may be also be concerned that you may lose the progress you have made, or worry about having a relapse in the future and your panic attacks return.

Often people have questions such as:

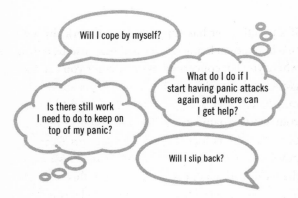

Will I cope by myself?

What do I do if I start having panic attacks again and where can I get help?

Is there still work I need to do to keep on top of my panic?

Will I slip back?

Once you begin to feel better, understandably you would want to maintain the positive changes you may have put into place. It can be scary to think of slipping back and having those intense, frequent and unpredictable physical sensations again.

Remember: Just having those scary thoughts about slipping back can be enough to kick off your vicious panic cycle again, and you start experiencing the very same physical symptoms you are scared of having. As you have now hopefully realised from using this book, this is quite a 'trap' and what people call a 'self-fulfilling prophecy'.

If a practitioner has supported your work through this book, then being discharged may also be a time where you get concerned as to whether you can face going it alone without that support. As above, this may be another 'scary' thought that might kick off your vicious panic cycle. The key thing to remember, however, is that it wasn't the support from the practitioner that helped you feel better. It's mostly the hard work you have put into using this self-help book and applying the skills you have learned that has done that. Through your hard work you have learned the skills needed to help get on top of your panic and you can successfully apply these again in the future if you need to. If needed, using this Toolkit in the future will help you keep things on track.

When someone has got on top of their panic, it is understandable they don't want to experience frequent, uncontrolled panic attacks again. This can mean they begin to look for any signs and symptoms that their panic disorder is returning and may misinterpret how they are physically feeling, their thoughts, or changes in their behaviour, as signs that things are slipping back into a relapse. However, as we have mentioned above and discussed fully in Section 2, it's normal to experience physical sensations in our body, and we should expect that this will happen at times. If you're going through a stressful time, say at work or in your personal life, you may even have several episodes of those intense and unexpected physical sensations in your body, and then possibly worry you have lapsed.

However, a lapse doesn't mean you have relapsed. Taking it easy on yourself when you have a lapse is important. At times we all act according to how we are thinking or feeling inside. It's when this has become a pattern that you fall into regularly and when you've got stuck in that vicious panic circle that it becomes a problem. Recognising a lapse for what it is and ensuring you don't lose hope that things will improve again is key.

IMPORTANT: Lapses may happen so the best thing is to recognise them for what they are and not as a sign you've gone back to square one.

You have the tools to ensure a lapse does not become a relapse by taking a step back and using Your Panic Diary to try and identify the things associated with the experience of the physical sensations that may have kicked off your 'vicious cycle' again. If you find yourself once more having greater belief that these intense and unexpected physical sensations mean there is something seriously wrong with you, then it may be a good idea to go back through Section 3 and apply the techniques again. This may help you get on top of your panic attacks before they take hold and possibly develop into panic disorder.

Hopefully, as you will have learned from using this self-help book, the techniques are there to 'help you help yourself' and can continue to be put into action if you feel you need to. You now have these skills should you ever need them again. Just like any new skill, if you note yourself slipping then you may need to practise the skills you have learned again. This will hopefully help you keep on top of your 'panic attacks' and spot any signs that you may be slipping back, or indeed 'falling forwards' into panic disorder. The good news is that by making a 'Relapse Prevention Plan' and putting this plan into action reduces this likelihood. It will also help en-sure you have the confidence to spot any 'red flags' to help you keep on top of your panic.

You can think of this section as a Toolkit to help you:

- Recognise the red flag type thoughts or situations that may be leading you to have those intense and unexpected physical sensations in your body

- Consider the things that have set off your vicious panic circle. For panic attacks, consider your experience of the physical sensations in your body. For panic disorder, also consider what helped to maintain those physical sensations to keep you in your vicious panic cycle

- Practice an approach to enable you to challenge a belief that the return of these physical sensations must indicate there is something physically wrong with you

- Know where to get further help and support again in the future should you need it

---

What's the difference between a lapse and a relapse?

A lapse: A lapse is a brief return to responding to your physical sensations associated with fear in the way you previously did. In particular, this could mean thinking again there is something physically wrong with you, monitoring your body for any sign that the physical sensations are returning and fearing their return. At times, thinking in this way is perfectly normal, the sensations may catch you out or occur at a time you are tired. As long as you don't let these physical sensations and the ways you respond to them take hold again, and you put back into practice the techniques learned in this book you can get back on track. Just don't give up and let these physical sensations take control again!

A relapse: Relapses occur when you completely return to your old ways of responding to your physical sensations associated with fear (and if you once again begin to experience them frequently). This results in you thinking and behaving in a similar way to how you did before. It is also likely that your belief that having these physical feelings must mean there is something physically wrong with you has crept up again. Often when a relapse occurs it is easy to think of it as a total setback and forget the skills and techniques that helped you before.

Unfortunately, we can't guarantee you will never experience physical symptoms associated with fear again. In fact we can guarantee you will; we all experience these on occasions and they can actually help to keep us safe. However, if you find them once again having a big impact on your life, you experience them more and more often, or you find yourself once more having greater belief that there is something physically wrong with you, then this is a sign that you need to do something about them. This is when it's time to put into action the things that helped before, which this self-help book will help you do. The key thing is to spot these signs earlier and put the Toolkit you are now going to create into action.

My early warning signs

The first step in thinking about the future and dealing with any setbacks is to think about the things you noticed when you began to experience panic. We understand you may not want to dwell on these or think about them now you are feeling better. However, we really encourage you to spend some time thinking about these, as they are the same things you may notice starting to come back in the future. If you notice them and then take action, hopefully you can get on top of them before they begin to take hold and have an impact on your life.

The vicious panic cycle below will help you. In the diagram below, write down the things you noticed first in three main areas:

- The **physical symptoms** you noticed first.

- The changes you noticed in **what you did** more or less of as a result.

- Any changes to the type of **thoughts** you had.

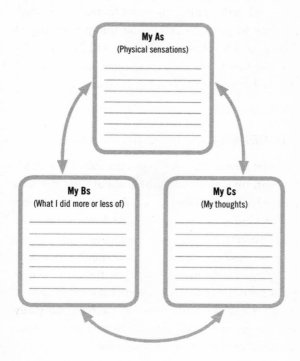

Red flags I noticed when I first experienced panic

When completing the vicious circle diagram, you may want to turn back to the one you completed at the start of the book. Think about the time when you first felt unwell, before it got to the point where you decided to seek help. You may find it useful to speak to someone close and ask if there were any early signs they observed in you. Often, other people start to see the changes in us before we do. They may have some really good insights, such as noticing you giving up things or no longer going places you used to enjoy. Or they may have become aware of you getting increasingly worried about what the physical sensations in your body meant.

My Red flags:

My early warning signs are:

_____

_____

_____

_____

_____

_____

_____

_____

_____

_____

_____

_____

If you, or someone you share your relapse plan with, spot signs that things on this red flag list are creeping back, it's a good time to begin taking action. Use the Panic Diary and Exposure that helped you before, so that the Vicious Panic circle cannot take hold again.

How things have improved since the start of treatment

Reflecting on your progress and how things have improved is also an important part of relapse prevention. So in the box below list some positive changes you've noticed that things are improving for you.

_____
_____
_____
_____
_____
_____
_____
_____
_____
_____
_____

Now, in the boxes over identify a few positive ways that progress in the things listed above is having on the following areas of your life:

Your family life

Your work life

Your friendships

Your social life

Things around the home

Re-rating my goals

At the start of this book we asked you to set some goals for yourself. If you did, re-rate these again using the worksheets over and compare the progress you have made in each area.

My goals for feeling better

Goal 1: ....

....

....Today's date___/___/___

I can do this now (circle a number):

0	1	2	3	4	5	6
Not at all		Occasionally		Often		Any time

One month re-rating   (Today's date___/___/___)
(circle a number):

0	1	2	3	4	5	6
Not at all		Occasionally		Often		Any time

Two month re-rating   (Today's date___/___/___)
(circle a number):

0	1	2	3	4	5	6
Not at all		Occasionally		Often		Any time

Three month re-rating   (Today's date___/___/___)
(circle a number):

0	1	2	3	4	5	6
Not at all		Occasionally		Often		Any time

Goal 2: ....

....

....Today's date___/___/___

I can do this now (circle a number):

0	1	2	3	4	5	6
Not at all		Occasionally		Often		Any time

One month re-rating   (Today's date___/___/___)
(circle a number):

0	1	2	3	4	5	6
Not at all		Occasionally		Often		Any time

Two month re-rating   (Today's date___/___/___)
(circle a number):

0	1	2	3	4	5	6
Not at all		Occasionally		Often		Any time

Three month re-rating   (Today's date__/__/__)
(circle a number):

   0   1   2   3   4   5   6
Not at all   Occasionally   Often   Any time

Goal 3: ....
....
....Today's date__/__/__

I can do this now (circle a number):

   0   1   2   3   4   5   6
Not at all   Occasionally   Often   Any time

One month re-rating   (Today's date__/__/__)
(circle a number):

   0   1   2   3   4   5   6
Not at all   Occasionally   Often   Any time

Two month re-rating   (Today's date__/__/__)
(circle a number):

   0   1   2   3   4   5   6
Not at all   Occasionally   Often   Any time

Three month re-rating   (Today's date___/___/___)
(circle a number):

  0   1   2   3   4   5   6

Not at all   Occasionally   Often   Any time

Once you have measured your progress, take time to reflect upon how far you have come towards reaching these goals. Are there other things that have improved too?

What helped things to improve

What treatment techniques did you use that helped you move toward getting on top of your panic? These form a really important part of your Toolkit for the future. List them here:

....

....

....

....

....

....

....

The Wellbeing Action Plan

The other really helpful strategy we recommend you undertake is to develop a Wellbeing Action Plan to help you review your Toolkit. To do this you should set some time aside weekly, or at least each month, to become your **Wellbeing Day**. Having a Wellbeing Day will help you identify your red flags earlier, and ensure you keep on top of the techniques you have learned in this book so that, should you need them, they are still fresh in your mind.

Keeping an eye on my panic attacks
Review date:
What has my panic been like this week/month (delete as applicable)?

Reading through my red flag list of early warning signs, have I had any that concern me?

Have I got any signs of:

- Fearing having the intense and unexpected physical sensations?   yes/no

- Actively monitoring or looking out for physical sensations in my body?   yes/no

- Avoiding doing things or going places?   yes/no

- Having thoughts that these physical sensations mean I am seriously ill or may even die?   yes/no

Do I need to take any action now to keep on top of my panic?

If so, what helped before from my Toolkit?

What do I need to do and when am I going to do it?

If things are going well – what is it that's been helping? Write in the vicious panic cycle things you're doing in each area that are helping to keep you on track

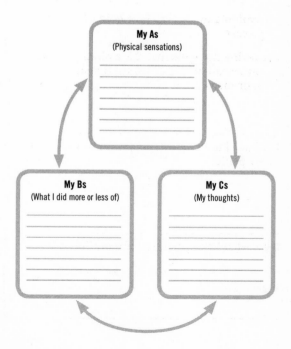

Keeping the skills I've learned in this book fresh

What are the key points involved in keeping a Panic Diary or engaging with the Exposure techniques?

Even if you are feeling well, take a few moments to read through Section 3 again to remind yourself about the key points of Exposure – and steps needed to carry it out. This is a great way to ensure you know what to do if you need the skills again.

Do I feel confident I know when and how to use the Panic Diary or to engage with the Exposure techniques again if I need to?

What is the main aim of the Panic Diary and the way in which Exposure works?

Date of my next review day:..

Put it in your calendar or somewhere you'll see it as a reminder.

Date:..

Is there still anything you would like to work on?

Sometimes there are areas you may still like to see change in. These may be goals you set at the start of treatment that you would like to work on further or perhaps things you would now like to do.

What do you still want to do?

How will you do it?

When will you do it?

Are there any resources you need to do it?

What things may get in the way of doing it and how can you overcome this?

Top tips from others

Below are some tips from other people who have worked through this book and professionals who have used a panic diary or exposure to get on top of their panic.

Top tip 1	'The best way to prevent a lapse is to keep practising your CBT skills! If you are regularly practising, you'll be in good shape to handle whatever situations you're faced with.'
Top tip 2	'Know your red flags. Watch for the times you feel more stressed or when things happen in your life. I shared my red flags with my wife and she sometimes notices before I do when my vicious panic cycle is starting again and reminds me to look through my Toolkit.'
Top tip 3	'Use your wellbeing action plan even if you're feeling well. It will remind you to look after yourself by setting time aside for you.'
Top tip 4	'Put your review day on the calendar each month in a coloured pen so that you know it is time for your review, or leave a Post it note on the fridge.'
Top tip 5	'Take it easy on yourself! At times everyone experiences unexpected physical sensations and they may actually be helping to keep you safe! So when you experience them, ask yourself "Am I doing something or was there a thought that just went through my head that may account for these panicky feelings?"'

Top tip 6	'Focus on the present moment! If you notice you're having worrying thoughts about the panic attacks returning, then try to do another activity that focuses your attention. It can help you stop worrying and help you feel better.'
Top tip 7	'Think about small changes you can make that add up to the big changes you may still want to do. Think of the big change as the end of a journey. Even when it feels a long way away, every little part of the journey gets you nearer to where you want to be, and taking these steps makes sure you're still heading in the right direction.'
Top tip 8	'Rather than thinking solely about the things you may still want to do or improve, also take the time to think about how far you've come.'
Top tip 9	'Use your Toolkit as often as you need to and have a weekly or monthly review day that you stick to. Unless you think it would be helpful, you don't need to review things every day, and remember that everyone experiences unexpected physical sensations at times. These are normal and OK, in fact sometimes they may be keeping you safe!'

Getting further help if you need it

Sometimes if you've put into place all the options you can, you may still feel you require additional support to get on top of your panic attacks or panic disorder. Knowing where and how to get help is a good thing to have in your Toolkit.

Where can I get more help?

Think of a good and trusted friend. Could you share this Toolkit with them so they can help you watch for your red flags? They will then also know what you need to do to feel better. Write the name of someone you can identify who could be your Toolkit supporter:

....

Fill in your GP details here:

Surgery address:

....

....

....

....

Telephone number:

....

....

Also see the further resources at the end of this book for details of other useful support organisations.

Congratulations

You've come so far to reach this point, and we are delighted you stayed with the book. Look what you have achieved as a result! Reflect on the progress you have made toward the goals you set at the start. We know it may not have always been easy, and we cannot take any of the credit for you feeling better. That's all down to you! You alone are the reason you are feeling better! We just provided the tools to help you to help yourself. It's down to the work you did using the techniques covered in this book. Be proud of what you have done.

The relapse prevention section will help you keep feeling this way. It will make sure you know when to put the tools back into action, should you ever need to. The book is always here should you need it.

In the next section we return to Mike and Ria to hear how they used CBT self-help to get on top of their panic attacks and beat their panic disorder, and to stay well. You may have already read their stories earlier in the book. You may want to write your own story in a similar way. This would be a lovely reminder of all the work you've done. Then, if you ever need to do more self-help, you can re-read it, knowing you did it before and can do it again. Many people have found this a really helpful thing to do.

Others have written themselves a short letter celebrating how much better they feel. Then they ask a friend or relative to post it back to them in three months' time. It becomes a surprise reminder of what they've accomplished and can do again if they ever need to.

We have also provided a further Resources section at the back. This has blank worksheets and details of useful information sources about panic and its treatment.

Good luck with your next steps and remember you have the skills to help yourself get on top of your panic!

Paul and Marie

RECOVERY STORIES

Mike's Story

Mike, the carpenter who you met on page 30, experienced panic attacks and used a Panic Diary and a CBT technique known as Exposure to feel better. Here is Mike's recovery story. His completed worksheets are here, along with details of what he did. Although Mike's situation may be different to your own, it will help you understand your own panic attacks and how to plan and carry out Exposure.

"Everything was good in my life, until I was about twenty-six. I had a steady job, my lovely wife Sue and two great daughters. I had always been in the best of health and even played football for Ashton Rangers, my local team. However, all of a sudden I started to get these terrible physical feelings in my body and had no idea what was happening to me. I thought about what could be causing them but nothing sprung to mind. OK, I was a bit more worried about earning money now Sue had given up work and we had Martha, my new daughter, but in this day and age we all have money worries, don't we? Sue was getting worried about me too as I was now getting these feelings a few times a month and she kept trying to get me to see the doctor. But I just wanted to carry on and hope they went away.

I had a steady job for a while, working with a large building firm to renovate a block of flats, so all my money worries were much smaller. OK, I had started to miss the odd day, but the guys on the job were fine about it as I always managed to make the time up when I felt better. However, it was a Sunday afternoon when it all happened and I could take it no longer. I had a really bad night the night before when I suddenly woke up having these terrible physical feelings in my body again. I was panting for breath, felt like I was choking, dizzy and sweating really badly. I just lay there and Sue was trying to get me to calm down. After about ten minutes Sue had enough and was going to call an ambulance, but luckily just when she was looking for the phone these feelings went away. I still had to convince her not to phone and, after a bit of a debate, she finally listened to me. After beginning to wonder if I was 'going crazy', I finally got back to sleep and all was fine. But the next day, it really happened.

Surprisingly I woke up after a disturbed night's sleep and felt really good, even more so as Sue had cooked me a full English breakfast. It was a lovely morning so we all decided to take the dogs out for a walk. We live in the country and at the back of my house there's a large field and if you walk through you get to a wood and walk through that. I had done the walk many times and the dogs really loved it, especially when they chased the rabbits. It was about ten minutes into the walk when, all of a sudden, it started again; I started to breathe really quickly, was really sweaty and was feeling like I was going to choke. I sat down as I became really dizzy and started to wonder if I was going crazy after all. And then something really strange happened; it was almost like I was outside my own body, sort of there but not there. This time I got really scared and Sue did as well because we were so far from anywhere and the mobile phone didn't have a signal. So we all sat there for what seemed like for ever, but must have only been about fifteen minutes, and then the awful feelings in my body just seemed to get better. After another five minutes, when all seemed OK again, we decided to walk back to the house. On the way home, Sue insisted this time she was going to make an appointment to see Dr Burkes, our GP, but if I got any more of these feelings this time she would phone for an ambulance right away with no arguments. But there were no arguments from me this time. Having these physical feelings whilst asleep and in the middle of a field, I thought, could only mean this was a serious medical problem.

On the Monday I went to see the GP and, as I expected, he checked my blood pressure and listened to my chest. I prepared for some bad news. However, to my surprise, he said everything seemed fine and began to chat to me about other things. He asked me if I was worried about anything at the moment and how I was doing at work, and at home with the new baby. Initially, I felt a bit stupid talking about myself like this, but he got me thinking when he asked me about work. Over the past few months I had started to feel a bit uneasy and unsettled at work, which was unusual for me. I had always loved working and not wanting to go in, or not really enjoying it when I was there, was unusual. I had even started to not enjoy the drive in now I had to go via Allington to get to work, a route I had always avoided as I didn't really like driving over the bridge there. I was surprised when the doctor started to ask more and more questions about work, and even more surprised when he said that maybe I was experiencing 'panic attacks'.

We both tried to think about what could be causing them and whilst we were none the wiser, he suggested I look at a self-help book called *How to Beat Panic Disorder One Step at a Time*. He said that a while back another of his patients was experiencing these and she found the book really helpful in understanding her panic attacks and she actually managed to sort them out. He said that initially something called a Panic Diary would help me see if there was anything obvious setting my panic attacks off. He then said that sometimes just being aware if there was anything setting them off could help, but if not then there was also something called Exposure that I could try. He also said however, that it would be good to keep in touch whilst I was using the self-help book just to see how things were going and he asked me to make another appointment in a month's time. This would be long enough to at least get hold of a copy and begin to use it.

Initially, I was very sceptical about the sound of all this 'self-help'. If I could have helped myself then I would have done that already. However, when I got home and told Sue what had been suggested, no sooner had I finished talking about the self-help book, that Sue got me and the kids in the car, drove us into town and, thankfully, the book shop had a copy in stock. I remember being very surprised at just the number of self-help books they had, covering a lot of different types of problems and thinking that there must be something in this. When we got home I started to read the book and got really interested reading about some of the ideas of what caused panic attacks. I was especially interested to find out how they could be caused by a number of things, including being related to the way our bodies have evolved and that they were even common in people who were asleep. This helped me feel a bit better but although this helped to explain a few times when I had panic attacks, there were many occasions it did not explain.

Over the next week I decided to complete the Panic Diary to see if there was anything obviously setting them off, but was still at a complete loss as to what this could be. During the next few days I kept the diary and used it to record a number of things when I experienced a panic attack. I kept the diary for another week or so, having to use more than one worksheet as I seemed to have lots to record. Interestingly, however, there seemed to be a clear pattern in what I was putting in my diary, with the same things appearing a few times.

My Panic Diary

Situation or object causing fear	Where were you, when was this, who were you with?	What was the thought (if there was one) about the situation or object going through your head *just before* you noticed your physical sensations?	Physical sensations associated with panic	Intensity of these physical sensations (0–100)	What do you fear about these physical sensations (what do you think will happen)?	Have you noticed anything about the situation or object that may have set your physical sensations and panic off?
Driving to work over Allington Bridge.	In car alone, driving to work on Tuesday.	'Oh, it's a bit windy today I hope this bridge does not sway too much.'	Shallow breathing, shaky, bit sweaty and feeling a little cold.	70	I think I'm going crazy and am a bit worried that I am having these feelings again, they can't be good for me.	I think it may be the bridge, I often feel like this when I have to drive over this bridge but never realised just how much I hate it.

Working on site, and having to repair some windowsills.	In flat 402, working alone.	'Oh, I don't like feeling like this, I feel a bit wobbly and it's horrible being so close to the window, blimey it's a long way down.'	Shallow rapid breathing, dizzy, shaking, felt liked being choked.	90	I'm really scared that all this panic is making me very ill, and being dizzy so near to the window is really dangerous, what if I collapse?	It's not all the time, sometimes working in these flats is no problem, but I really don't like working in the higher ones. I wonder if it's something to do with the height?
Driving over the bridge again.	Car alone, driving to work on Wednesday.	'Here go the feelings in my body again, I hate this bridge.'	Rapid breathing, sweaty, shaky, cold.	75	I wish these feelings would stop, they must be making me ill, I must be going crazy.	OK I'm sure it's the bridge, I don't feel this way when I can avoid it but always when driving over it.

On site at work again, and once again near the window.	Flat 214, working alone.	'Oh, I'm getting dizzy again.'	Bit dizzy, rapid breathing, bit shaky	55	I just don't like feeling like this and am sure it can't be doing me any good.	I felt bad again, but looking above, it was not as bad this time, but interestingly was at a lower flat this time.

Intensity of Physical Symptoms Rating Scale

0	10	20	30	40	50	60	70	80	90	100
No Intensity					Moderate Intensity					Worst ever Intensity

Even from looking at the Panic Diary worksheets I began to notice a few things but wanted to continue completing the self-help book properly. So I began to write the things I noticed that set my physical sensations off in the 'Things That Set Off My Physical Sensations' worksheet.

Next, I looked at what I had written in the 'Things that set off my physical sensations' worksheet and wrote these into the worksheet 'Panic Cycle Ladder' in the order that related to how much fear they caused me. The situation or event causing me most fear was written at the top and the one causing me least fear at the bottom. To begin with I also included 'Working in a ground floor flat' that I had rated as 20 on the Fear Rating scale, but then remembered that I should only include those things scoring at least 50.

The final step of my Exposure Plan was by far the scariest. I had to begin to face the things I had written in my Panic Cycle Ladder. To begin with this seemed overwhelming and initially I started to chicken out. I really didn't want to set these physical sensations off on purpose, I really hated having them and they were beginning to scare me more and more as I started to worry about what may happen to me if I keep getting them. However, Sue could see I was getting really worried and, over a cup of tea,

Things that set off my physical sensations

Situation or object causing fear	Fear Rating (0–100)
Driving over Allington Bridge.	70
Driving over Allington Bridge but with Sue.	50
Asleep, woke up in a panic again, was not aware I was even dreaming.	85
Working by the window in a flat on a higher floor.	90
Working by the window but in lower-floor flat.	55
Working in a ground-floor flat.	20

Fear Rating				
0	25	50	75	100
No Fear	Mild Fear	Moderate Fear	Severe Fear	Full Panic

LEVEL OF FEAR	SITUATION/OBJECT CAUSING FEAR	FEAR RATING (0-100)
	Working by the window in a flat on a higher floor.	90
Most fear	Asleep, woke up in a panic again, was not aware I was even dreaming.	85
	Driving over Allington Bridge.	70
Medium fear		
	Working by the window but in a lower floor flat.	55
Least fear *(but at least 50 as far as possible)*	Driving over Allington Bridge with Sue.	50

chatted to me about the possible benefits of facing my fears. She also said she had seen something like this on television, helping a person to get over their fear of spiders, and said it really worked. In the end the person even had a spider running over the back of her neck! I was still very uneasy about doing this but Sue helped me begin to complete the next work-sheet, **Facing Your Fears**.

To begin with, I was to choose the thing from the Panic Cycle Ladder that I had written as causing me the least (but still 50%) fear, which was 'Driving over Allington Bridge with Sue'. I was a bit unsure if this was acceptable as a first step as it seemed it may break Exposure rule 2: *Without Distraction*; one of the Four Rules of Exposure. I discussed this with Sue, and whilst it was possible that I found driving over the bridge easier when Sue was there as she helped distract me, I could not think of anything better to start with, and it still caused me 50% fear, even if Sue was helping to distract me. So we decided to start with this exercise, but that we should make sure others were without distraction.

When I thought about the Four Rules of Exposure again, I spotted another difficulty with this exercise, this time related to Exposure rule 3: *Prolonged*. Usually when driving over the bridge, it takes me no more than ten minutes, often less when I can speed up to get over it. However, Exposure rule 3: *Prolonged* indicated that I needed to stay in the situation until my fear had dropped by 50% of what it was at the beginning of the exercise. This really got me thinking, but once again Sue came up with a possible solution. She said that maybe there was somewhere to pull in on the bridge where I could stop the car and sit in it for long enough to do the Exposure exercise. I had no idea if there was, as when driving over the bridge I tended to be so focussed on all those physical sensations in my body, so Sue said she would take a drive to the bridge and find out. When she got back she said there was a place I could pull in and sit in the car for long enough for me to do the exercise. So I wrote all this in the **Facing Your Fears** worksheet and began to prepare to actually face my fears on Saturday. I wrote the date and time I planned to do the Exposure exercise on the worksheet and waited, with some stress, for Saturday to come. Saturday morning came and the first thing I did was to rate my fear between 0–100 as I began to prepare for the Exposure exercise, rating it as 20, but this went right up to 60 at the start of the exercise. I then started the exercise and Sue set the timer on her watch to see how long it would take for my fear to drop to at least 30, half what it was at the beginning of the exercise. I must admit I thought that we may be there all day, but 45 minutes later my fear had dropped to 30 and we could stop the exercise. I can't say it was much fun really, not only being terrified but sitting in a car a bridge, and then not even being able to talk to Sue. But I was glad I did it, as it was good to see how these physical sensations dropped in enough time. I was also glad Sue was with me the first time. Not only did I find it a bit easier with her there, but she had also thought of everything. For example, she managed to get her mum over to look after the kids each day we needed to do this; I would never have thought of that!

I repeated the exercise another five times, as informed by Exposure rule 5: *Repeated*. Each time it tended to be a little bit easier and I was pleased to say on session 6 my fear hardly went up at all when preparing to do the exercise and only went as high as 20 even at the start of the exercise, coming down very quickly, only taking five minutes! This was very much more manageable and we decided that I should now move to the next Exposure exercise: written in the Panic Cycle Ladder 'Working by the window but in lower-floor flat'.

Over the next few weeks, I kept going and kept to my Exposure Plan, continuing to face my fears for each of the things I listed in the Panic Cycle Ladder, working my way up from the bottom to the top. Each time I created a new Exposure exercise, I ensured I

Facing Your Fears worksheet

Exposure exercise

To drive to Allington Bridge with Sue, park in the parking bay halfway over the bridge and wait there for long enough until my fear drops by half. Also, I should not talk to Sue as this may distract me too much.

Date and time you will do your next exposure exercise		Exposure Fear Ratings (0–100)			
		Preparing for Exposure exercise	Start of Exposure exercise	End of Exposure exercise	Duration of Exposure exercise
Sat 16 May	Session 1	20	60	30	45 mins
Sun 17 May	Session 2	20	55	30	40 mins

Mon 18 May	Session 3	15	50	25	40 mins
Tue 19 May	Session 4	10	40	15	30 mins
Wed 20 May	Session 5	10	30	15	20 mins
Thur 21 May	Session 6	5	20	10	5 mins

Comments

I was terrified at the thought of having to do this, but although it was difficult I was surprised at how quickly my physical sensations sorted themselves out. They were the same physical sensations I have been having a lot of with the panic attacks, but they went away all on their own, and the time it took them to go away dropped right down, doing this just six times. I want to do it a couple more times, but I'm really happy with this. If all is good I will move to the next exercise on my Panic Cycle ladder: 'Working by the window but in lower-floor flat'.

Fear Rating

0	25	50	75	100
No fear	Mild fear	Moderate fear	Severe fear	Full panic

followed the Four Rules of Exposure and each time it was all quite similar, although the starting point for the fear was higher and it took longer to come down. On one occasion it took 1 hour and 10 minutes the first time I did my top Exposure exercise: 'Sitting on the window sill in a top-floor flat'. The final time I did the Exposure exercise: 'Sitting on the window sill in a top floor flat', my fear only went as high as 25 at the start of the exercise and then only took ten minutes to get as low as 10. I was really happy with this, especially when Sue said at times even she feels a little dizzy when in a high place, that most people do.

Finally I had got to the top of my Panic Cycle Ladder and could drive to work and even work on the top floor and have none of those unexpected and intense physical sensations. More generally the panic attacks I had in other places also seemed to get better. Since finishing the exercise in the self-help book, things have been much, much better. I have not woken up having a panic attack now for nearly a year since finishing the book, and the dogs are much happier now I am able to take them for walks through the fields again, chasing those rabbits. Obviously, sometimes when stressed I still get some of those physical sensations in my body again, but now I am much better able to understand why I get them and what they are related to.

For example, even now when walking through the fields on occasions, I can feel the physical sensations beginning to be set off again. But I am now much more aware of what these are likely related to and they seem to disappear very quickly, mostly not even lasting a minute.

In fact I have embraced so much of what I have learned from using this book that I decided to face the biggest fear I could possibly think of, and one I previously never dreamed I would be able to do. As a bit of a celebration for getting over my panic attacks, and also landing a new contract job on a housing estate, I decided to take Sue and the girls for a weekend break in Blackpool. Whilst there, I took Sue and the girls to Blackpool Tower and we all did the 'Walk of Faith', where you walk out onto a glass floor panel near the top of the tower and look at Blackpool beneath your feet. It was a little bit scary, indeed scary for us all, but it was a great feeling walking into the middle and just standing there and looking down. I think Sue was a little more scared than I was, and Martha did not stop crying the entire time she was on the glass panel. I think she was likely hungry, unless of course this was down to evolution again!**”**

Ria's Story

You met Ria on page 31, who, after getting more and more frequent and intense panic attacks, was diagnosed with panic disorder. After seeing her GP, she was referred to a Psychological Wellbeing Practitioner and they began to work through this self-help book. Here is Ria's story, which picks up during her treatment. It will help you see how completing a Panic Diary helped her understand and get on top of her panic disorder, and how she made a recovery plan to help her stay on top of her panic.

❝Until about twelve months ago I was really enjoying life, just like any single twenty-year-old should be. I had a good social life, loved going out with my mates drinking and dancing, and although one day I was hoping to settle down, I didn't have a regular partner; I was still enjoying myself far too much for that just yet. I also really loved my job in Blackwood Hospital where I had worked since leaving school. I was the personal assistant to a lovely older doctor called Dr Bashan. I had worked for Dr Bashan since joining the hospital, and he was really great, being very patient with me, kind and supportive. He had even promoted me three times since starting a couple of years ago as an administration assistant. As I say, everything was really great until I started to get these terrible physical feelings in my body, my heart would race a bit and I would start to become a bit jittery and have these hot flushes.

To begin with I put them down to stress that I knew a bit about. Whilst at secondary school I struggled a bit with anxiety and had even seen a school nurse. She chatted to me about anxiety and gave me some things to read and it really helped actually. I got to understand that these awful feelings I had in my body were caused by my stress, something about our bodies releasing a chemical when we get stressed to allow us to run away, fight or freeze and do nothing, in response to things that cause us fear. The school nurse said this used to be a really helpful response a very long time ago when we lived alongside dangerous animals, but whilst our bodies still respond this way to things causing us stress, often such things are more related to schoolwork or things like that.

So this 'fight, flight or freeze' response was on many occasions not helpful, but we still had it, it was part of the way we were made. So to begin with I was able to put these awful physical feelings down to this.

However, about twelve months ago I started to experience these physical feelings more and more frequently, and once, at work, my colleague Deidre was aware of me having one at my desk. She said I may have been having a 'panic attack' and said that her son had experienced these. This started to get me thinking and I began to wonder if they might be related to something physically wrong with me but held onto the idea that they were stress-related. I was becoming a little more stressed at work as Dr Bashan had announced he was retiring and maybe it was something to do with this. However, these 'panic attacks'; a racing heart, feeling sick, hot and shaky began to get much worse and lasting longer than they did before. I remember one particularly bad panic attack at work where I was just leaving but got so dizzy I had to sit down and grip the desk really hard to even avoid falling out of the chair. And it must have lasted about twenty minutes as I missed my bus home. After that I became a bit more convinced that there must be something seriously wrong with me and started to keep an eye out for those feelings in my body. I even stopped doing things I had done, giving up jogging and leaving much earlier for the bus to work so I didn't need to rush. I was now really, really worried about getting another panic attack and was keeping a very close eye on my physical feelings. Then the following night was the last straw. Although I had been OK during the day and all seemed OK when I went to bed, a few hours later I woke up having a really bad panic attack; all those physical feelings just seemed to kick off. They just started, and couldn't be down to any stress as I was asleep and I wasn't even dreaming. My mum could hear me crying as I was really scared now. She just sat with me holding my hand, until about twenty minutes later they just seemed to sort themselves out. However, I was so terrified that Mum stayed with me all night, and I am a grown woman!

The next day, Mum phoned the GP practice and told them about what happened to me during the night, but still they said they couldn't fit me in until the Wednesday. I was a bit angry and decided the best thing to do was to take the day off and stay in bed. I was surprised at how much I slept, I must have been really exhausted but was really glad that just lying there wasn't putting any strain on my body, just in case they were causing these physical sensations. Finally Wednesday came, and with Mum we went to see my GP, Dr White. She asked me a few questions, took my blood pressure and took some bloods. I was glad she checked me over and all seemed fine, but got a little annoyed (as did Mum) when Dr White said she needed to send the results off and made an appointment to see me for the Friday.

The next few days were terrible again, I was having these panic attacks more and more frequently and took the time off work, which made me a bit worried as Dr Bashan had now left and the new doctor had started. What would he think of me? I was now having the panic attacks what seemed like every five or six hours and, although intense, every time me or Mum was on the verge of calling an ambulance they got better; but I was now wondering if having these panic attacks meant I could be dying. Finally Friday arrived and we went to see the GP again and get those blood results back. I was so glad Mum came with me, not only for support but I simply don't know if I could have caught the bus on my own. To my surprise, Dr White told me that the blood results showed nothing at all; in fact they were of someone who seemed in the very best of health. She took my blood pressure again but said all was as it should be there as well. Mum and me were just so relieved, but we both could not understand exactly what was going on. Why was I getting these terrifying physical feelings?

Dr White then mentioned that she thought I may be experiencing panic disorder, but that there was something she could do to help. She mentioned a referral to someone called Amanda, who worked in the practice and could help with problems like this. I was still unsure about all this, but, as Mum said, it's much better at least there being something available that may help. The next day this Amanda phoned me at home (I was still off work) and said she had someone drop out and if I wanted she could fit me in for an assessment in a couple of weeks. Two weeks later I went along with Mum. Amanda introduced herself as a Psychological Wellbeing Practitioner (or PWP for short) and said that she was able to support people with a range of anxiety problems and depression. But first she needed to do an assessment to really try to identify what the problem was.

Amanda assessed me and said that as the GP had suggested, it did seem I was struggling with something called panic disorder. She then explained that when we become stressed our bodies release something called adrenaline and that it's a perfectly natural process and could actually keep us safe. I knew this, as I had been a worrier most of my childhood. I also said this time things were different; the physical sensations often lasted longer, were far more frequent and I even had them a couple of times when I was asleep. Amanda seemed to understand what I was saying and discussed a few things about panic disorder with me, but also said the very best thing she could suggest was that

I started to work through a CBT self-help book. It would give me a lot more information about panic disorder and help me understand why I was getting them more frequently and why they were lasting longer. She even said CBT self-help was suggested for use in the NHS now, which made me feel a bit better as I knew all about NICE recommendations because of my job and had even heard about CBT. I was also glad that Amanda said she could help me use the book weekly and said she could offer meetings in the GP practice or could also support the book over the telephone. This sounded strange to me at first, but indeed would make things a lot easier because I could make appointments for after work so I wouldn't need to take even more time off. I was getting a bit stressed about that because my new boss, Dr Salter, had started at work.

On the way back home from the GP practice, Mum stopped in town to pick up the book, which I started to read that very night. I began to understand a bit more about panic disorder and the difference between panic attacks and panic disorder and things that helped to make panic attacks turn into panic disorder, and in fact I was doing a lot of these things. I was checking my body all the time and monitoring my physical sensations and on its own this did cause me to be stressed more often. I had also given up most things that exerted my body just in case they set them off. Indeed I was feeling a little upset as I was now not jogging and had put on some weight. Initially, when reading the first few sections of the book, I still had some questions. For example, why was I getting these terrible physical feelings at night and what was setting them off previously, before I was getting them all the time? I had another terrible night that night after waking up with all those terrible physical feelings in my body again. They went away after five or ten minutes, but this time I felt so awake I decided to have a read of the self-help book in bed and I'm glad I did.

I understood what the book was telling me about panic disorder but things still didn't fully make sense, such as what was setting off the panic attacks in the first place. The book, however, went on to talk about keeping a Panic Diary and how this could help me recognise the things that set off my panic, any thoughts that went through my head just before I had them and what I did when I had them. It also asked me to think about what I feared when having panic attacks and then got me to think about what could have been setting off my physical feelings and panic attacks. Whilst it seemed I had to do quite a lot keeping the Panic Diary, and I was even a bit worried about doing it in case it showed me something worrying, I decided to give it a go and started the Panic Diary that day.

My Panic Diary

Situation or object causing fear	Where were you, when was this, who were you with?	What was the thought (if there was one) about the situation or object going through your head *just before* you noticed your physical sensations?	Physical sensations associated with panic	Intensity of these physical sensations (0–100)	What do you fear about these physical sensations (what do you think will happen)?	Have you noticed anything about the situation or object that may have set your physical sensations and panic off?
Was a bit late to work this morning as a bit tired and had to rush,	Rushing to bus stop on way to work on my own.	'Oh, no, I'm running late and rushing to work. What if these physical	Heart pounding (but could be me rushing!), shaky, sweaty, sickness.	65	I think that because I am rushing and my body is already being pushed	Well, I was rushing to the bus and beginning to experience physical sensations but this

pushing my body a bit more than I had done recently.	feelings get set off again?'				it may set off a panic attack.	could always be the bus I guess as I am unfit at the moment, but a bit concerned about what will happen.
Walking into work a bit late after missing the bus.	Going into department at work and seeing new boss	'Oh no, there's Dr Salter, I hope he doesn't get too angry with me, I have only been back two weeks and late already.'	Shallow rapid breathing, heart pound-ing, bit shaky, choking.	60	As above, really I am wondering if these physical feelings are kicking off again.	Well I was clearly worrying, wasn't I?! I thought a lot of my worry was behind me, but wonder if I am still a little prone to get stressed.

| Woke up from sleep having a panic attack. | Alone in bed. | Initially 'Oh hell, they are off again', but soon thought about what I had read and calmed myself down. Said to myself "It's OK, just think what you read!" | Rapid breathing, sweaty, shaky, cold. | 85 | Initially I was taken by surprise, but then thought about the book, and calmed right down, don't think the panic attack meant anything really, just that I am human. | I remembered that people can get panic attacks in their sleep for no obvious reason, and quickly calmed down, and interestingly, the physical sensations disappeared very quickly, a minute? |

Intensity of Physical Symptoms Rating Scale

0	10	20	30	40	50	60	70	80	90	100
No Intensity					Moderate Intensity					Worst ever Intensity

I had another three or four panic attacks that day, but found completing the Panic Diary really helped and got me thinking. I carried on filling the diary out for the next three weeks. But I was really glad that the panic attacks were getting less and less frequent. At the end of each week I looked back over what I had read and it was very interesting to see things there in black and white. I could see that many were associated with work, in particular my new boss and doing things wrong. And over the past few weeks I had done a few things wrong, for example when I forgot to cancel a patient's appointment and forgot to pick up some patient medication from the pharmacy. But Dr Salter was very nice about it. OK, he was a bit annoyed when the patient turned up and started shouting in the waiting room, but then again who wouldn't have been? But he had a chat to me the next day and was really supportive. He said he could see I was a bit worried at times, but also said he had heard great things about me from Dr Bashan, and would see how things went but he was thinking of training me up in a new patient database system they were thinking of using. I was really, really, pleased and felt a bit stupid that I was worrying so much once again, especially as Dr Salter was such a nice boss.

The next week, during my telephone support session, I was discussing what I had learned from my

Panic Diary with Amanda the PWP. As usual she took the questionnaire scores for depression and anxiety and said that the scores were now normal and given I was no longer having frequent panic attacks, no longer worried about what they meant, and had even started jogging again, that we could think about ending the support sessions. She said she felt I had got on top of my panic disorder. However, she did say she wanted to make one last session for the next week to go through 'Relapse Prevention' and directed me to Section 4 of the self-help book. At first I was a bit reluctant to do this and said to Amanda that I really felt much better now so couldn't I just have this as my last session. But she urged me to complete Section 4 and have the final session next week, so in the end I agreed. Over that week I was really glad I persevered and completed the section on relapse prevention. It was really helpful to think about things that could indicate I was slipping back into panic attacks again; my Red flags.

Ria's Red flags:

Worrying about what the physical sensations mean.

Thinking really extreme thoughts, such as I may collapse or even be dying.

Stopping doing things in case I exert myself too much.

Taking time off work.

Watching and monitoring my body for every little sign that something bad may be happening to me.

I also set up a Wellbeing Action Plan to set a date to keep check of my panic attacks and ensure all was still well. This was really good as it helped me appreciate that the number of panic attacks had reduced right down. In fact, I was rarely having 'panic attacks' any more but was still getting those physical sensations associated with stress from time to time. I was still getting a bit stressed at times but not this time about those physical feelings, but more everyday stresses, especially those related to work. I started off reviewing them each week, but after a couple of weeks decided to do it monthly instead.

Keeping an eye on my panic attacks

Review date: Wednesday 13th June

What has my panic been like this ~~week~~/month (delete as applicable)?

They've been much better over the last month. In fact I would not say I have had any 'panic attacks'. I have been stressed at work a few times with all those physical sensations kicking off, but these were very much related to stresses at work. Last week I was really quite stressed as I was on a training course to learn a new patient database and a bit scared I would not be able to learn it. But I was fine – I even helped someone else in the end!

Reading through my red flag list of early warning signs, have I had any that concern me?

No, things have been much better.

Have I got any signs of:

- Fearing having the intense and unexpected physical sensations?
  ~~yes~~/no

- Actively monitoring or looking out for physical sensations in my body?
  ~~yes~~/no

- Avoiding doing things or going places?
  ~~yes~~/no

- Having thoughts that these physical sensations mean I am seriously ill or may even die?
  ~~yes~~/no

Do I need to take any action now to keep on top of my panic?

No, I just need to remember what I know from this book and keep the learning fresh in my mind.

If so, what helped before from my Toolkit?

Not applicable.

What do I need to do and when am I going to do it?

I just need to remember what I have learned from this book. Also if I begin to get a bit worried about my physical feelings again, then I will keep a Panic Diary again, it helped so much last time. However, I am noticing myself becoming more of a worrier again; I am often having those physical sensations, especially at work. But I know that they are more related to my stress and worry at work. I wonder if there is anything I can do to sort these out as well? So I am going to check out the NHS Choices website at the weekend that I had seen mentioned in the self-help book to see what it has to say about anxiety more generally.

During my final support session with Amanda, we went through my Relapse Prevention Toolkit and what I had written. Amanda was really pleased with just how much I had done and how I was now aware of the things causing me to have panic attacks, or as I now liked to call them, just those stressy physical feelings. She was also impressed with how much understanding I now seemed to have about the things I did and thought that turned panic attacks into panic disorder.

Well at the time of writing my story, all this was over a year ago and I'm pleased to say I have only experienced one more 'panic attack'. I woke up in the middle of the night having one, but as I know now this simply happens sometimes, I don't feel it even counts! I have obviously been stressed quite a few times, but to some extent I put this down to maybe this is just me. However, I did check out the NHS Choices website on anxiety that was listed at the end of the self-help book and it was really interesting. I sometimes think that maybe I might still have a bit more of a problem with anxiety than other people and have thought about possibly trying another self-help book or getting other help to see if it could help. At the moment, however, I am just keeping an eye on this. I have come a long way in the past year or so and am once again enjoying life at work (well, most of the time) and being back out with my girlfriends. However, I hate to say it but my circle of friends seems to be getting smaller all the time with them getting married and things like that. Maybe it's my time to start to think about settling down, but I guess I will need to meet Mr Right first. **"**

FURTHER RESOURCES

My Panic Diary

Situation or object causing fear	Where were you, when was this, who were you with?	What was the thought (if there was one) about the situation or object going through your head *just before* you noticed your physical sensations?	Physical sensations associated with panic	Intensity of these physical sensations (0–100)	What do you fear about these physical sensations (what do you think will happen?)?	Have you noticed anything about the situation or object that may have set your physical sensations and panic off?

Intensity of Physical Symptoms Rating Scale

0	10	20	30	40	50	60	70	80	90	100
No Intensity					Moderate Intensity					Worst ever Intensity

Things that set off my physical sensations	
Situation or object causing fear	Fear rating (0–100)

Fear Rating				
0	25	50	75	100
No Fear	Mild Fear	Moderate Fear	Severe Fear	Full Panic

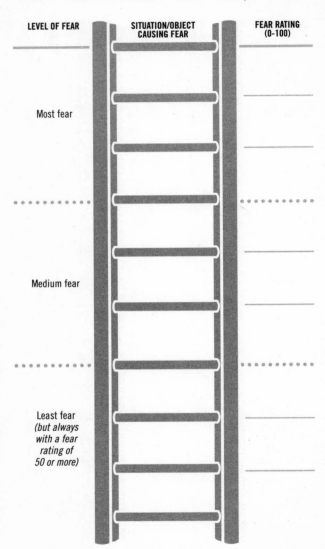

LEVEL OF FEAR

SITUATION/OBJECT
CAUSING FEAR

FEAR RATING
(0-100)

Most fear

Medium fear

Least fear
*(but always
with a fear
rating of
50 or more)*

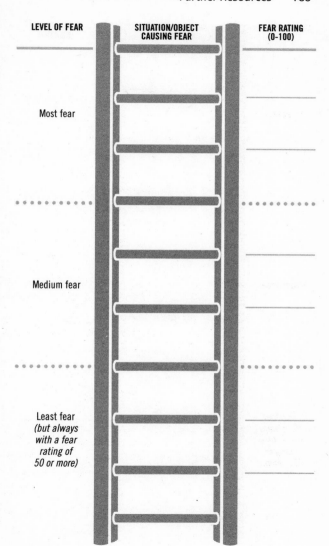

| LEVEL OF FEAR | SITUATION/OBJECT CAUSING FEAR | FEAR RATING (0-100) |

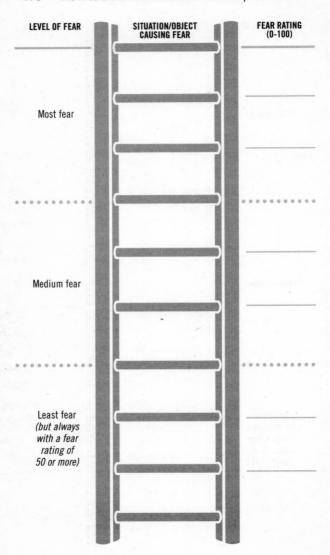

LEVEL OF FEAR

SITUATION/OBJECT
CAUSING FEAR

FEAR RATING
(0-100)

Most fear

Medium fear

Least fear
*(but always
with a fear
rating of
50 or more)*

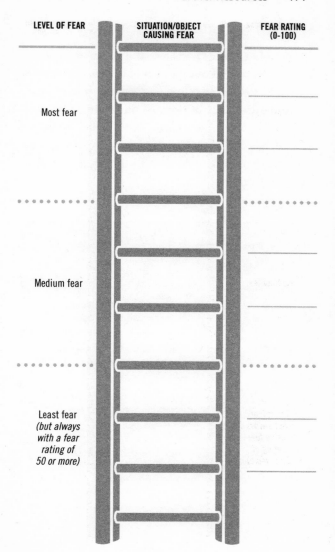

LEVEL OF FEAR

SITUATION/OBJECT
CAUSING FEAR

FEAR RATING
(0-100)

Most fear

Medium fear

Least fear
*(but always
with a fear
rating of
50 or more)*

Further information

The NHS Choices website has a range of excellent resources to find out more about panic attacks and panic disorder. They include a video that discusses the experience of both of these difficulties and provides useful information about them, including some helpful tips. There is also information on medications recommended by NICE for treating panic disorder.

You can get more information about panic at the following websites www.	
Panic Disorder	http://www.nhs.uk/conditions/panic-disorder/pages/introduction.aspx
Panic attacks	http://www.nhs.uk/conditions/stress-anxiety-depression/pages/understanding-panic-attacks.aspx http://www.nhs.uk/conditions/stress-anxiety-depression/pages/ coping-with-panic-attacks.aspx
Medication	http://www.nhs.uk/conditions/ssris-(selective-serotonin-reuptake-inhibitors)/Pages/Introduction.aspx).

Sometimes when people get treated for one specific emotional difficulty they become aware of other stress- or anxiety-related difficulties they may have been struggling with. If this is the case for you, then this website contains further information you may be interested in.

http://www.nhs.uk/conditions/anxiety/pages/introduction.aspx

Support

Talk to your GP who may be able to help you access a range of services that deliver support for CBT self-help. In England, the Improving Access to Psychological Therapies (IAPT) programme provides specialist support for CBT that is available either as supported self-help or more traditional face-to-face therapy. You can self-refer into IAPT services so you can make an appointment direct, without first having to go through your GP if you would prefer to do that. Although, as discussed earlier, even if you would prefer to access the IAPT service directly you are still advised to let your GP know if you start treatment. You can find the location and contact details of your nearest IAPT services at the following website by typing in your current location:

http://www.nhs.uk/Service-Search/Psychological-
therapies-(IAPT)/LocationSearch/10008 www.

Similar services to IAPT are now being developed in Scotland, Wales and Northern Ireland. So, if in these countries, check out the availability of support for CBT self-help at your GP practice, if you would like to work that way.

In addition to the support available through your healthcare provider, there are also a range of charitable or voluntary organisations that offer support groups, some of which are run by people who have experienced panic disorder themselves. There is a national charity called 'No Panic' which provides support for carers and people who suffer from panic, alongside support for a wider range of anxiety related disorders.

http://www.nopanic.org.uk www.

Options available for support include a mentor service, recovery groups and a helpline, some of which are run by people with first-hand experience of panic. Alternatively, groups local to your area may be available and you may be able to find information about these from your GP practice, from the library, or perhaps check them out on the Internet.

If you are feeling suicidal

If you are feeling suicidal and having thoughts of ending your life, this can be really scary and distressing. Please tell someone how you are feeling and get the right support in place. These thoughts and feelings do not last for ever and your mood will improve. Suicide is not the answer. Please remember that these thoughts are just that, thoughts. They can just pop into your mind when you are feeling down and low, so can take you by surprise. Speak to your GP or another healthcare professional urgently.

The Samaritans can be contacted via email, the phone or in person at one of their branches. Their volunteers are available 24 hours a day and will always pick up the phone. They can provide a listening ear and advice in times of crisis. Their contact details are overleaf.

	Contact details for the Samaritans in case needed in times of crisis
Website	http://www.samaritans.org/ how-we-can-help-you/contact-us
Telephone	116 123
Post	Freepost RSRB-KKBY-CYJK, PO Box 9090, Stirling, FK8 2SA

You can also find more information about feeling suicidal and what you can do to get support on the NHS Choices website.

http://www.nhs.uk/conditions/suicide/pages/
introduction.aspx

DEDICATIONS AND ACKNOWLEDGEMENTS

Paul:

I would like to dedicate this book to all those who help me to keep me going and enjoying my work, leisure and family life. Big thanks go to my wife Paula, children Oliver, Ellis and Amélie for their patience and smiles and to my wider family: my mum Muriel and big sisters Julie and Wendy, who at times have also demonstrated a fair bit of patience. I would also like to offer sincere thanks to the Exeter and Honiton dialysis units at the Royal Devon and Exeter Hospital. Their clinical expertise, flexibility, support and the odd cup of tea serve as an example as to how far the medical treatment of people with chronic kidney failure has come, enabling people with renal failure, like myself, to continue to lead a very full and active professional, working and family life and to make a difference where they can. They serve as a true example of the best the NHS has to offer, and long may it last.

Marie:

I would like to dedicate this book firstly to my father John Montague Chellingsworth (1 February 1937 – 8 December 2015) who sadly passed away during the writing of this book. He was a true inspiration through his own thirst for knowledge and his encouragement. Secondly it is dedicated to all the practitioners and patients I have had the privilege to work with over the years.

INDEX